Markham's Brotherhood

The Rosicrucian Manifestos in Modern English

Markham's Brotherhood : The Rosicrucian Manifestos in Modern English

© 2019 Steven E. Markham

Foreword © 2019 Robert T.L. Hughes

All rights reserved, including the rights to publish this book or any parts thereof, in any form. The moral rights of the author have been asserted.

No part of this book may be reproduced or transmitted in any form or by any means, graphic, electronic or mechanical, including but not limited to photocopying, recording, photographing, or by any information storage and retrieval system or otherwise without the written permission of the author, except where permitted by law.

Use of images on pp. 70, 72, 76, 78, 82, 86, 92, 94, 102 by kind permission of the Wellcome Collection (CC by 4.0)

Published by Ferret Books

First Edition - 2019

ISBN: 978-1-9160345-0-1

For Fra. R.T.L.H., Fra. D.C.M.,

Sor. S.E.M., Sor. S.D.

Contents

Foreword	9
Overture	13

Fama Fraternitatis — 21

Chapter One: Thomas Vaughan's Introduction — 23

Chapter Two: *Fama Fraternitatis, or, A Report of the Fraternity of the most laudable Order of the Rosy Cross* — 29

Chapter Three: Return to Europe — 37

Chapter Four: The Brotherhood — 43

Chapter Five: The Tomb — 51

Chapter Six: To a New Brotherhood — 63

Confessio Fraternitatis — 69

Preface — 71

Chapter One:
Confessio Fraternitatis or The Confession of the Laudable Fraternity of the Most Honourable Order of the Rosy Cross — 73

Chapter Two - Fourteen — 75-104

Chemical Wedding: Christian Rosencreutz 105

Chapter One: The First Day 107

Chapter Two: The Second Day 121

Chapter Three: The Third Day 145

Chapter Four: The Fourth Day 183

Chapter Five: The Fifth Day 207

Chapter Six: The Sixth Day 223

Chapter Seven: The Seventh Day 245

Chapter Eight: The Eighth Day? 259

Acknowledgements 261

Foreword

The *Fama Fraternitatis*, The *Confessio Fraternitatis* and the *Chemical Wedding of Christian Rosenkreutz* are the foundational Manifestos of the Rosicrucian movement. Anyone who claims to be a student of Rosicrucianism ought therefore to be familiar with the content and import of these texts.

The first English translation of the *Fama* and *Confessio* was published in 1652 by the Welsh clergyman and alchemist Thomas Vaughan (under the name of Eugenius Philalethes). Since then the "Vaughan Translation" has been the primary text for the English speaking student of Rosicrucianism.

Vaughan's text (as in its original German) is highly discursive with multiple nested clauses – a literary style considered a virtue in his time but a vice in ours. Issues over the accuracy of the translation aside, the text is further hampered by careless punctuation and its presentation without paragraphs, rendering it a labour of concentration for the modern reader.

The sheer effort of reading Vaughan's text has challenged the determination of many a student such that I believe not many who consider themselves students of Rosicrucianism have persevered in reading the text with concentration from beginning to end.

It is the nature (sometimes by necessity) of the language of Western Esoteric literature to be – to a greater or lesser extent – as occult as its subject matter. Occult ideas obscured by metaphor and symbol are obstacles enough for any reader in search of the meaning of a text. However, while the language may be arcane, it need not be archaic.

For the benefit of the modern reader Frater Markham has rendered Vaughan's text far more amenable. The lengthy sentences have been shortened and more familiar terms and words have replaced the archaic.

For example, Vaughan's opening paragraph of The Fama comprises a single extended sentence containing so many clauses that it is difficult comprehend its content and import. There's just too much information to hold in mind while trying to complete the sentence.

Frater Markham has rendered the same in three distinct sentences, without loss of content or meaning and with a lexically judicious clarity which no longer challenges the reader's cognitive capacity.

While the reader of *Markham's Brotherhood* may continue to grapple with Symbol, Metaphor and Allegory, at least his attempts to do so are no longer hampered by simultaneously deciphering outdated language and style.

Frater Markham's translation of the Vaughan text into modern English therefore provides a welcome relief from this impediment and a much needed help for the earnest Rosicrucian student and the casual reader alike.

The present volume also includes Frater Markham's translation of the *Chemical Wedding of Christian Rosenkreutz* (first published in English by Ezechiel Foxcroft in 1690), which is similarly rendered more congenial to the modern reader.

I have no doubt that for those who have previously abandoned the effort of reading these fundamental and important texts on account of their antiquarian style, *Markham's Brotherhood* will encourage the reader to revisit them and rekindle their interest in the Rosicrucian sphere of the Western Esoteric Tradition.

I am honoured that Frater Markham has invited me to provide this foreword to his *"Brotherhood"* having spent many pleasant hours in his company discussing its progress. I must confess however, that while playing no part in Frater Markham's translation itself, it has been my privilege to be, at times, a ready ear for his ideas, an anvil for the hammer his of analysis and - mostly - a voice of reassurance in the value of the enterprise and of encouragement in the completion of his labours.

Frater RTLH

Overture

'Have you read the Fama?'

This is a question I have heard many times in Rosicrucian company. Almost always, I heard that cruel little inner voice of mine say 'Yes, but I bet you haven't'.

The reality here is that the damned thing is almost unreadable. At best, it can be painfully struggled through and some semblance of meaning extracted. If you can stay the course, there is a fascinating story within the archaic English and almost impenetrable sentences (I speak here of the 'Vaughan translation', which is still the commonly owned version). The truth is that it is not generally read at all and if it is, perhaps once. The reader is asked to contend with sentences such as this:

'The same Song was also sang to him by other Nations, the which moved him the more (because it happened to him contrary to his expectation,) being then ready bountifully to impart all his Arts and Secrets to the Learned, if they would have but undertaken to write the true and infallible Axiomata, out of all Faculties, Sciences and Arts, and whole Nature, as that which he knew would direct them, like a Globe, or Circle, to the onely middle Point, and Centrum, and (as it is usual among the Arabians) it should onely serve to the wise and learned for a Rule, that also there might be a Society in Europe, which might have Gold, Silver, and precious Stones, sufficient for to bestow them on Kings, for their necessary uses, and lawful

purposes: with which such as be Governors might be brought up, for to learn all that which God hath suffered Man to know, and thereby to be enabled in all times of need to give their counsel unto those that seek it, like the Heathen Oracles: Verily we must confess that the world in those days was already big with those great Commotions, laboring to be delivered of them; and did bring forth painful, worthy men, who brake with all force through Darkness and Barbarism, and left us who succeeded to follow them: and assuredly they have been the uppermost point in Trygono igneo, whose flame now should be more and more brighter, and shall undoubtedly give to the World the last Light.

That is two hundred and fifty six words in a single sentence, with a bit of Latin thrown in for good measure…

It is no surprise that few beyond the committed enthusiasts and those of an academic leaning could get through such prose. Most people's understanding is from notes and summaries rather than the texts themselves. It is also not particularly lyrical in its form, which also reduces the reward for the struggling reader.

What I wanted was a readable Modern English version of the Vaughan translation. One that could be given to those interested in Rosicrucianism and read through without needing to decipher every line. A book that could be picked up, read a little, put down again and returned to without losing track. I had many discussions about this with my good friend Rob Hughes, bemoaning the fact that, yet again, someone we knew had either given up on the Fama, not read it at all or had claimed to have read it but obviously hadn't. Finally, I decided to stop talking about it and try to create the book that I wanted to see.

I made many attempts over many years and chipped away at it from time to time. To be honest, I continually talked myself down as to the value of the work, doubting that I would actually produce anything of worth. And so, I left it for long periods of time and worked upon it infrequently over the course of years. As the work progressed, I became frustrated at several points as I could not quite figure out the actual meaning of certain passages and phrases. I mentioned this to Rob, who responded with 'What does it say in the German?'. As ever, he cut straight to the heart of the matter (I love him for this). It opened up a whole new angle that I had been blind to: I had only thought of the job as translating Vaughan and neglected the fact that it was derived from the German publications and manuscripts! Taking a few of the problematic passages, I compared them with early German printings. Success! I managed to make sense out of excerpts where I had previously failed. I then began a process of another pass through the entire text, referring more and more to the German sources as I did so. I immediately came across several anomalies where the German text seemed to say something quite different to the Vaughan translation. I checked, as best as I was able and ended up referring to several German and English translations and manuscripts to try to clear up these anomalies. But they remained. The German was most certainly different to the Vaughan version. In some cases, better academics than I had commented on this in books and papers and only confirmed my 'discovery'.

I was now faced with a choice; to continue with a straight translation of Vaughan or to include the corrections in the narrative, rather than as annotations. I confess that I moved back and forth several times. On one hand, the Vaughan translation, correct or not, was the one responsible for the large majority of English-speakers' understanding of Rosicrucianism. On the other hand, the German manuscripts are the earliest source documents but this would steer me away from my primary objective of 'readable Vaughan'. I ultimately decided to present the original texts as closely as I could and record the mistranslations and relevant differences as annotations to the main text.

I continued with this, making multiple passes through the Fama until it started to take a form that I would describe as 'reasonably readable'. I decided to also work on the 'Confession' and it was a short step from there to decide to complete the trilogy with the 'Chemical Wedding'.

I make no great claims of scholarship in my versions of these documents. I have tried to be as accurate as possible and to not misrepresent the original intent of the Fama and Confession. In the case of the Chemical Wedding, it is more about the storytelling but, again, I have tried my best to keep as close to the original as I could - no matter how weird…

My primary aim was to create a readable version of the three original Rosicrucian 'manifestos'. I hope that I have done so.

Conventions

I have decided to use the translation 'Brother' to represent Fr (Frater) throughout and 'Brotherhood' rather than Fraternity. Although Frater is a nice term to use and will be familiar to most readers, I feel that Brother is more accessible to the entire modern readership. In the same way I have used 'Founder' in place of Father in some places and translated 'Cloyster' as Monastery rather than 'Cloister', as the term will be unfamiliar to many. I have also translated the word Axiomata as 'principles', as this seems to me to be the best modern representation, which keeps the intent. In the Chemical Wedding, I have taken '*Jungfrau*' as 'Maiden' rather than 'Virgin'. I have applied the capitalized version 'Maiden' to one of the central characters whilst her attendants and other minor characters are referred to as 'maidens'.

In the *Fama*, I have divided the text into chapters for ease of reading. These, together with the chapter headings, are my own and do not appear in the original work.

Annotations

I have chosen to give notes at the end of any chapter that contains annotations. This is to avoid a single, large list in an appendix and to allow the main text to flow more freely. As there are extensive explanations in some cases, I felt that notes on page footers would be obstructive and have opted for what I hope is a convenient manner of presenting this information to the reader.

The Fama

The initial translation was based upon the 1652 Thomas Vaughan English translation. The main German documents I have referenced are the 1617 Frankfurt printing and the 1614 Kassel printing, as well as the Wellcome Library manuscripts. I have also referred to various other manuscripts and editions.

Christian Rosencreutz/Rosenkreutz/Rosenkreuz

As there were many different forms of 'Shakespeare' for example, so a name such as Rosencreutz also has different forms.
The *Societas Rosicruciana In Anglia* records it as 'Rosencreutz' in its Zelator ritual as well as in one section in its 2015 directory and then 'Rosenkreuz' in the same document, referring to its CCR award. It is also commonly written as 'Rosenkreutz', which is an Anglicised

version of 'Rosencreutz' (I tend to use this form myself). *AMORC* tends to use 'Rosenkreuz' and 'Rosencreuz' is used by the *Societas Rosicruciana In America*.

However, the use of the 'k' spelling variants can become confusing when the abbreviation CRC is also used.

Notably though, the full title of the Rosicrucian document 'The Chemical Wedding' was first published in 1616 as '*Chymische Hochzeit Christiani Rosencreutz anno 1459*'. It is then a small step from 'Christiani Rosencreutz' to 'CRC'.

It is not specifically mentioned that the Fama refers to Christian Rosencreutz as his name is never fully given. Many commentators have inferred this from using CRC and RC in their texts. However, the original German does not always use this form; for example '*Ch. Ros. C*. This original form offers much stronger evidence for it being Rosencreutz and, together with references to the 'Confession', which does name him, makes it almost certain that the Fama refers to him.

I have opted for 'Rosencreutz' in this book for consistency although, even today, it seems that all variants are still in common use and are interchangeable.

Thomas Vaughan

Thomas Vaughan was a clergyman from Brecon, Wales. His version of the Fama Fraternitatis, which he published in 1652 is the one best known to the English-speaking world and the majority of modern Rosicrucians. It is not known who translated the Fama from the German texts. Vaughan says in his preface that it *'belongs to an unknown hand'*. I refer to this version as 'Vaughan' throughout for ease of reference.

Vaughan took his translation of the *Fama* and *Confessio* from English manuscripts that were already in circulation. Vaughan also added a lengthy preface to his edition, which I have not translated here, regarding this as his own work and unconnected with the Rosicrucian Manifestos. However, I have included and modernized his shorter 'Introduction' to the book in recognition and deep appreciation of his part in bringing these works to English-speaking Rosicrucians.

Fama Fraternitatis

Chapter One

Thomas Vaughan's Introduction

To the Wise and Understanding Reader.

Wisdom, according to Solomon, is an infinite treasure to man. She is the breath of God's power and a pure influence that flows from God's glory. She is the brightness of eternal light and an untarnished mirror of God's majesty, reflecting an image of His goodness.

She teaches us moderation and thoughtfulness, goodness and strength. She understands the subtlety of words and answers ill speech. She foresees signs, wonders and future events.

This treasure was given to Adam, the first man and father: Therefore, it appears that, after God had given him the beasts of the earth and the birds of the air, Adam named all the creatures, according to their apparent nature.

After the fall into sin, this beautiful jewel of wisdom was lost and darkness and ignorance came into the world. However, in spite of this, the Lord God still, on occasion, gave the gift of wisdom to His friends.

Wise King Solomon told us that he received the gift of wisdom from God after prayer. Then he understood how the world had been created and the nature of the elements. He understood the true meaning of time, the cycle of the year and the laws governing the stars. He learned the characteristics of domestic and wild animals and the weather. He understood the thinking of men and their intentions. He knew the biology of plants and roots and their uses.

Now, I do not think that there is anyone who would not wish with all his heart to be given such a treasure but this can only happen to those whom God chooses to receive wisdom, which he does by sending his holy spirit from above. We have therefore decided to print this essay, 'The Report and Confession of the Worthy Brotherhood of the Rose and Cross'[1], so it can be read by all - because it clearly shows the discoveries telling us what the world may now expect.

Although the story may seem somewhat strange and many may reckon it to be a piece of philosophical writing rather than a true history of the Brotherhood of the Rose and Cross, what is written here will show there is more to it than might first be imagined. What it all means will also be easy to understand by anyone (of at least a reasonable intelligence).

Those who are true disciples of wisdom and true followers of the spherical art will appreciate these things and realise the importance of studying them, as has been done by some notable people. Adam Haselmeyer, Public Notary to the Arch Duke Maximillian, wrote 'The Theological Writings of Theophrastus'[2] and 'The Jesuit'[3] where he proposed that every Christian should be a true Jesuit – that is, to walk, live, exist and remain in Jesus' name.

However, he did not find favour with the Jesuits because when he wrote in the Fama, he did not name the members of the Brotherhood of the Rose and Cross. The highly educated Jesuits took exception to the lack of information. They seized him and put him to work as a slave in the galleys; for which action they will no doubt receive judgement.

Blessed Aurora[4] will now begin to appear after the dark night of Saturn has passed and her brightness will eclipse that of the Moon and those small sparks of heavenly wisdom, which remain within men. It is a precursor of pleasant Phoebus[5] who, with his clear and fiery, shimmering beams, brings forth the blessed day long awaited by the true of heart. Then daylight will truly be known and the heavenly treasures of Godly wisdom and the esoteric secrets of the world will be revealed according to the beliefs of our forefathers and the wise men of ancient times.

These treasures will be the ruby, fit for a king and the shining carbuncle, which is said to shine and give light to darkness, to act as a perfect medicine for all imperfect bodies, changing them into purest gold and curing all of Man's diseases, easing pain and misery.

Reader, let me therefore urge you to pray earnestly to God with me that He may open the hearts and ears of all those who do not listen and grant them his blessing that they are able to recognise Him as all-powerful. Appreciate nature, whilst honouring God. Love, help, comfort and support our neighbours and heal the sick.

CHAPTER ONE: NOTES

[1] *'Famam & Confessionem, of the Laudable Fraternity of the Rosie Cross'*

[2] *'ex scriptis Theologicis Theophrasti'*

[3] *'Jesuiter'*

[4] Aurora - In Roman mythology the Goddess of Dawn

[5] Given as *'Phebus'* by Vaughan (Middle English spelling). Phoebus is the Greek 'Apollo' and God of the Sun.

Chapter Two

Fama Fraternitatis, or,
A Report of the Fraternity of the most laudable Order of the Rosy Cross.

Considering that the one wise and merciful God in recent times has given His mercy and goodness to mankind by enabling us to gain a more perfect knowledge of His son Jesus Christ and nature, we may rightly boast of this happy time where half of the previously hidden world is now revealed to us. He has also shown us many wonderful and never before seen works and creatures of nature and, more than this, has raised men inspired by great wisdom, who may revitalise and summarise all currently imperfect arts to perfection. Then finally, Man may understand his own nobility and value, know why he is called 'Microcosmus' and know how far his knowledge of nature extends.

The ignorant of the world will not appreciate this but will probably sneer instead. Scholars will never agree due to their pride and personal ambitions. But, if they were united, they might, out of all those things that God gives to us today, compile a 'Book of Nature'[6] and a perfect method of all arts. But, such is their opposition that they will not progress and stick to their old ways and praise the Pope[7] and also Aristotle, and Galen (who, if they were still alive would happily discard their faulty beliefs). They praise that which is only a fragment of knowledge compared with the clearly manifested light and truth.

These great weaknesses are no good for such a great work: Although theology, physics and mathematics side with the truth, nevertheless, the old enemy shows his cunning. He obstructs every good work with his slander and uses argumentative people and dreamers to hinder progress.

Our devout and enlightened Father, Brother C.R., a German and the head and founder of our original Brotherhood, worked for a long time to reform this situation. Because of his poverty (despite being of noble birth), he was sent to a monastery at five years of age. He learned both Greek and Latin adequately and his youthful enthusiasm caused him to pester one of the Brothers to let him join a pilgrimage to the Holy Land. His request was granted and he was put under the care of Brother P.a.L.[8].

This Brother died whilst in Cyprus and so never got to see Jerusalem. Our Brother C.R. did not return however, but decided to make his own way to Damascus, intending to continue from there to Jerusalem. Due to illness he was unable to complete the journey and so remained in Damascus, becoming popular with the Turks there because of his healing skills.

In the meantime, he became acquainted with the Wise men from Damcar[9] in Arabia and heard of the great miracles they had performed and their deep knowledge of all nature. The high and noble spirit of Brother C.R. was so inspired that he forgot about Jerusalem and made a bargain with the Arabians to take him to Damcar for an arranged fee.

He was only sixteen when he arrived but was of a strong German[10] constitution. The wise welcomed him, not as a stranger, but as someone they had long expected. They called him by name and, much to his surprise, told him secrets he had not yet learned about his own monastery! He learned the Arabian language to such an extent that, in the following year, he translated the Book M[11]. into Latin. This is where he learned Physics and Mathematics, which the whole world would celebrate if more love and less envy existed within it.

Enlightened, he decided after three years to return, sailing over the Persian Gulf into Egypt where he stayed for a short time, carefully noting the Plants and Creatures of the area. He then travelled the entire Mediterranean Sea to Fez, as he had been directed by the Arabians.

And it is a real shame for us, that wise men so far away from each other, are of the same opinion, hating all contentious writings, but are also so ready and willing to openly share their secrets with others[12].

Every year, the Arabians and Africans correspond about their arts, happily asking questions, consulting each other and sharing new discoveries or evidence to support or refute their reasoning.

Every year, something came to light and knowledge of mathematics, physics and magic (practised most skilfully in Fez) was improved.

Nowadays in Germany, there is no shortage of scholars, magicians, kabbalists, physicians and philosophers. It is a shame that there is not more love and kindness amongst them and that most of them do not share their knowledge.

At Fez, Brother C.R. was acquainted with those known as the 'Elementary Inhabitants'[13] who revealed many secrets to him. We Germans could similarly gather together many things like this, if there was a common purpose and desire amongst us.

He admitted that, in Fez, the Magic was not always pure and that the practice of Kabbalah was degraded by their religion. Nevertheless, he made the best use of it and strengthened his own faith in the harmony of the whole world throughout the ages.

CHAPTER TWO: NOTES

[6] *'Librum Naturae'*

[7] Vaughan uses 'Porphiry' here, which refers to the Neoplatonic philosopher, born in Tyre. This does not appear in the original German text at all, which uses 'Papst' or 'Pope'. This is consistent with the Fama's Papal criticism later on which uses the word Papst in the same form: *'they would have challenged the Pope, Mohammed, Writers, Artists and Philosophers more strongly'*.

[8] The 'Brother' undertaking the pilgrimage is described as Brother P.A.L. by Vaughan and Fr P.a.L in German translations and manuscripts. Other versions just call him 'a Brother'. I have taken the earliest German naming 'P.a.L.' for him. This form of the name seems to suggest a similar convention as that used by Phillppi à Gebella who signs himself as P. à G. in the (Latin) version of the Confession printed in 1615.

[9] Damcar is used here in the German and is distinct from Damascus in the text. However, there was much confusion, as the two seem to be used interchangeably to some extent. Vaughan commented on this in his Preface and stated that it '*hath indeed mistaken Damascus for Damcar in Arabia*'. In reading through the story however, the German text uses 'Damascum' (Damascus) and then 'Damasco in Arabia' (Damcar). It uses just Damasco after this. It seems clear (and makes narrative sense) that Brother RC shipped himself over to Damascus and later, having met the Arabian wise men who lived there, travelled to Damcar in Arabia. I have stayed with this narrative for this modern translation.

There is no specific location given for Damcar so it may be taken that either this name has been used as an alias for a real place or it is completely mythical.

[10] Vaughan says that he was of a 'strong Dutch constitution', which seems odd as CRC is described as being of German birth and descent. I originally thought that 'Dutch' may have been either a blanket description which included Dutch and German people, or a colloquialism. However, checking the German text, it says 'teutsch', which is an old version of Deutsch and so literally means 'German'.

[11] The book 'M' has been suggested as '*Liber Mundi*' (Book of the World) or '*Mysterium*' (Mystery)

[12] Vaughan has this as being shared 'under the seal of secrecy' however; the German text suggests that it was openly shared. This is one of several examples where Vaughan's version conveys the opposite meaning. It is fascinating that the English-speaking world has followed the opposite principles than those originally intended and it has come back to influence the original - I have found modern German versions which have changed the wording to suggest that secrecy was involved – this is <u>not</u> the case.

[13] 'Elementary inhabitants' probably refers to spirits or elementals as described by Paracelsus: *Just as visible Nature is populated by an infinite number of living creatures, so,*

according to Paracelsus, the invisible, spiritual counterpart of visible Nature (composed of the tenuous principles of the visible elements) is inhabited by a host of peculiar beings, to whom he has given the name elementals, and which have later been termed the Nature spirits. Paracelsus divided these people of the elements into four distinct groups, which he called gnomes, undines, sylphs, and salamanders. He taught that they were really living entities, many resembling human beings in shape, and inhabiting worlds of their own, unknown to man because his undeveloped senses were incapable of functioning beyond the limitations of the grosser elements.' Hall, M. (2003). *The secret teachings of all ages : an encyclopedic outline of Masonic, Hermetic, Qabbalistic, and Rosicrucian symbolical philosophy : being an interpretation of the secret teachings concealed within the rituals, allegories, and mysteries of the ages.* New York: Jeremy P. Tarcher/Penguin.

CHAPTER THREE

Chapter Three

Return to Europe

It is fair to say it follows that, as every seed contains a whole tree and its fruit, then likewise, every cell of man contains a whole world whose religion, policies, health, anatomy, nature, language, word and works are all as one; agreeing, aligning and in tune. Of the same melody as God, heaven and earth. Anything not aligned with this is error, falsehood and the work of the Devil who is solely the first, middle and last cause of conflict, ignorance and darkness in the world. Also, one may examine each and every thing on earth and find that everything that is good and right is always in agreement and harmony with itself but everything else is rife with a thousand conceited mistakes.

After two years, Brother R.C. left Fez and sailed into Spain with high hopes and many valuable possessions. He hoped that the scholars of Europe would celebrate his work and amend and organise their studies based on the solid foundation he had made.

Therefore, he conferred with the scholars of Spain, showing them the errors of our arts and how they may be corrected and where they should look for the signs of the times to come. He argued that these signs should align with those of the past. He pointed out how the faults of the Church and current ethics could be amended. He showed them new plants, fruits and animals, which did not align with the old philosophy[14] and gave them new principles by which to understand all things.

But they just laughed at him. It was all new to them and they were scared that their great reputation would be lessened if they admitted their mistakes. They were happy with things as they were and mocked 'He who loves disruption so much, let *him* change'.

He heard the same thing again and again from other Nations, which upset him even more, as it was so unexpected. He was ready to share all of his arts and secret knowledge to scholars of all faculties if they would only embrace the true and infallible principles of the sciences, arts and nature. He intended to direct them inwards, like a globe or circle, to the very centre (this method is common practice in Arabia) so it could be adopted by the wise and learned as laws. He also proposed that there should be a European Society, which would have gold, silver and precious stones in sufficient quantities to give to kings for necessary uses and lawful purposes. For example; to educate the rulers to learn what God requires them to know so they are able to give counsel at all times of need, like the heathen oracles.

Indeed, we must admit that the world in those days was in great upheaval and was striving for a solution. This brought forward strong and righteous men who broke forcibly through darkness and barbarism, leaving those of us who came after to follow them. They were the uppermost point of the triangle of fire whose flames are now brighter and longer and will most certainly give the last light to the world.

Theoprastus, was one of these men in both vocation and calling. Although he was not part of our Brotherhood, he had nevertheless carefully read the Book M. His great talent was enhanced by this but he was also hindered in his path by the same arrogance seen in many learned and seemingly wise men, so he could never discuss his views peacefully. This prevented him from passing on the knowledge and understanding of nature that he had gained.

And so, he made fun of these busybodies in his writings and did not show them his true self. Nevertheless harmony, as previously mentioned, is found in his work and he would no doubt have taught this to scholars had he not thought them so deserving of mockery rather than worthy of being instructed in greater arts and sciences.

Then, leading a carefree life, he finally ran out of time and left the world to its foolish pleasures.

But let us not forget our loving founder, Brother C.R.:

After much arduous travelling and futile attempts to share his true instructions (and because of the changes that would soon come as well as the strange and dangerous struggle that would follow), he returned to his beloved Germany.

There he could have bragged about his art, especially the transmutation of metal but he cared more about humankind, the citizens of Heaven, than he did about personal glory.

Nevertheless, he did build a suitable house for himself in which he contemplated his travels and philosophy and refined them as a true legacy in a memorial book. In this house, he spent a great deal of time on mathematics and made many fine instruments using all fields of art. However, very little of this survives - as will soon be made clear to you.

CHAPTER THREE: NOTES

[14] Here, we reach another point where the Vaughan translation gives the exact opposite of the original texts. Vaughan says that the new growths, fruits and beasts <u>did</u> concord with the old philosophy whereas in German this says the exact opposite - that they <u>did not</u> align with the old philosophy.

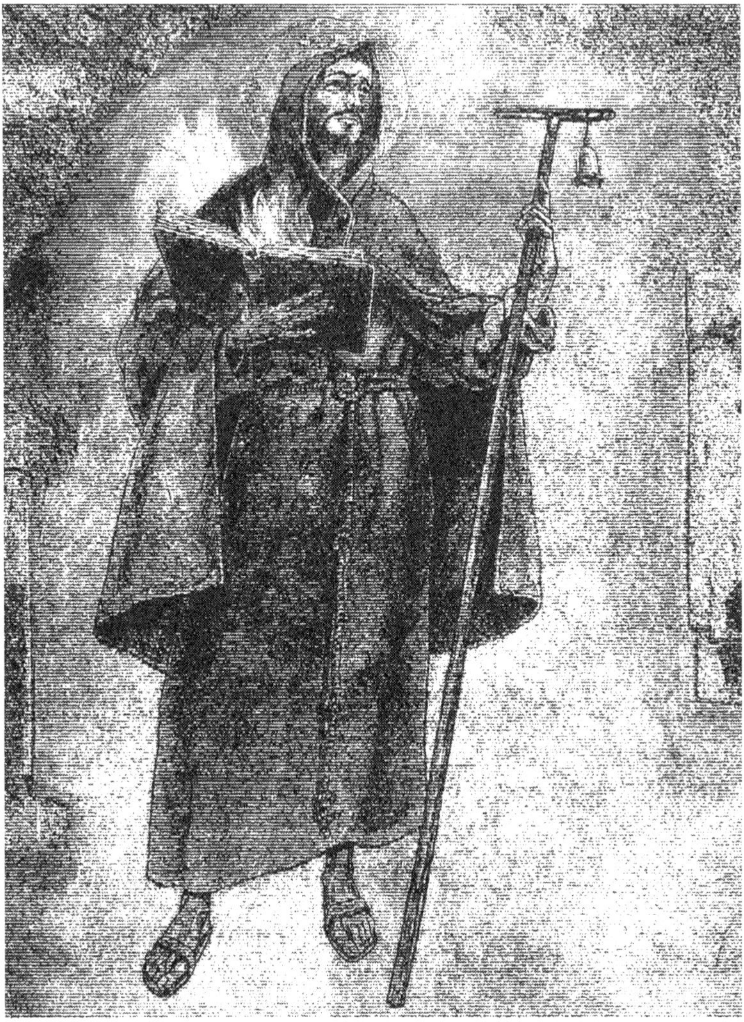

Chapter Four

The Brotherhood

After five years, he once again longed for reformation. Although he was strong, passionate and tireless, he doubted that he would find decent assistance. Undaunted, he still undertook the task alongside a few others. He still bore a great affection for his first monastery and chose three of his Brethren; Brother G.V., Brother I.A. and Brother I.O.[15] all of whom had greater knowledge in the arts than most others at the time.

He made them swear to him that they would be faithful, diligent and secretive and to commit themselves to carefully writing everything down, as per his instructions; so those who would come after them, being inspired to join the Brotherhood, would not be deprived of the least syllable or word.

In this manner, the Brotherhood of the Rosy Cross began; First, by four persons working together who made the magical language, writing and an extensive vocabulary which we still use daily for the praise and glory of God and in which we find great wisdom.

They wrote the first part of Book M but it was a monumental task. The large numbers of sick people coming to them hindered their progress so, as the new building (named *Sancti Spiritus* or 'Holy Spirit') was completed, they decided to recruit more candidates for the

Brotherhood. As a result they selected; Brother R.C. - his late father's nephew[16], Brother B., a skilled painter and G.G.[17] and P.D. - their writers. All of them were German with the exception of I.A. and they were now eight in total, every one of them bachelors, having taken a vow of celibacy. Together they compiled a volume of everything that man could desire, wish or hope for.

Although, admittedly, the world has changed a lot over the last century, we are certain that our principles will remain unchanged until the end of times. Even at the peak of its greatest and final age, the world will not achieve greater. For our cycle begins from the day that God said 'Let It Be'[18] and shall end when he says 'Perish'[19]; God's clock strikes every minute, whilst our own hardly strikes each hour.

We also firmly believe that, if our Brethren and Fathers had lived in our enlightened times, they would have challenged the Pope, Mohammed, writers, artists and philosophers more strongly, and would have been more constructive rather than critical, aspiring to their ultimate goal.

When these eight Brothers had completed and organized all things in such a way so that it needed little maintenance and were all sufficiently well taught and able to discuss and teach the secrets and philosophy perfectly, it was time for them to part. As they had agreed at the beginning, they divided themselves between several countries so that they could not only secretly impart their principles for scrutiny by scholars but that they themselves would be well-placed so that, if they observed anything significant or perceived an error, they may inform each other.

Their agreement was this:
1. None of them shall claim to do anything other than to cure the sick and this would be free of charge
2. None of them are obliged to wear special clothing – they will follow the customs of the country
3. Every year, on C. day they will meet at the 'Sancti Spiritus' or send apologies for their absence
4. Every Brother should look for a worthy successor
5. The word C.R. will be their seal, password and emblem
6. The Brotherhood will remain secret for one hundred years

They swore to follow these six rules and five of them departed. Brothers B. and D. stayed with the founder, Brother R.C. for a year before they too departed. Brother R.C. was left with his cousin and Brother I.O. who would stay with him for the rest of his days.

And although the Church was still not reformed, we know that it was still on their minds and we know what they longed for:

Every year they happily reunited and reviewed their activities; it must have been such a pleasure to be able to hear all of the wonders, which God had created throughout the world, told truthfully, clearly and without embellishment.

One can be sure that these people, joined together by God and the heavens and chosen from the wisest men, lived together in a bond of unity with great discretion and kindness towards one another.

In this commendable way, they spent their lives. They were free from disease and pain but, in spite of this, they could not exceed their allotted time, which God had given them.

The first of the Brotherhood to die was I.O. who died in England, as Brother C. had foretold a long time before. His servant followed him. He was an expert in the Kabbalah as his Book H. is proof: In England he is well known, mainly because he cured a young Earl of Norfolk of Leprosy.

They had decided that, as far as possible, their graves should be kept secret and, to this day, it is not known what became of some of them, other than every one of them was replaced with a worthy successor.

But, as God is our witness, we will confess that whatever secrets we have learned from the Book M. (although we see the image and pattern of the world before our own eyes) we do not know our fate nor our hour of death. That is known only to God himself who wants us to always be prepared.

Now, we shall continue with this in our *'Confession'*, where we will set out thirty-seven reasons why we are revealing our Brotherhood and freely sharing our mysteries without constraint or being rewarded. We also promise more gold than India and China could supply to the King of Spain - for Europe is pregnant and will deliver a strong child who will require a great gift from its godfather.

After the death of Brother O.[20] Brother R.C. did not rest but called the remaining Brothers together as soon as he could and (we assume) his burial was arranged. Before now, we (who are the youngest generation), did not know when our loving founder R.C. died and only had the bare names of the founders and their successors. Yet, there came to us a secret, passed on through hidden words concealed within the speeches of the last hundred and twenty years[21]. Brother A., the successor of D. (who was the last of the second circle and its successors) and had lived alongside many of us, passed this on to the third generation and its successors.

Incidentally, we have to admit that, after the death of Brother A., none of us knew the slightest thing about Brother R.C. and the first of the Brotherhood other than that which was written in our 'Library of Philosophy'[22]. This, amongst other titles, contained our 'Principles'[23] and works from the most elaborate 'Wheel of The World'[24] to the fruitful 'Proteus' [25]

Similarly, we do not know whether this second generation were of the same level of wisdom as the founders or whether they were admitted into every secret.

By the planning, tolerance and command of God, whom we most faithfully obey, we shall reveal to the reader what we have heard about the burial of Brother R.C. We want to record it faithfully so that, when we are contacted in a discreet and Christian manner, we will not be afraid to clearly and publicly print our names, surnames, meetings and anything else required.

CHAPTER FOUR: NOTES

[15] The three Brothers are often named here as GV, JA and JO in translations. The original German has GV, IA and IO so I have stuck with this version).

[16] The phrase '*Deceased fathers brothers son*' is used by Vaughan here and has been given esoteric meaning by many later commentators. The original German takes the form of '*son of the brother of his late father*'. As RC is referred to as a cousin later on, it seems that the actual meaning and intent is straightforward. Often the simplest explanation is the best…

[17] The English translation names this Brother only as 'G.'; I have taken the original German name, which is 'G.G.'

[18] '*Fiat*'

[19] '*Pereat*'

[20] The original German text says Fr O here rather than IO (It is usually JO in the English versions).

[21] The original German printing has 120 years (in numbers not words) whereas Vaughan gives it as 100 years as do the handwritten German manuscripts. I have, in this case, opted for 120 to make it consistent with the following discovery of the tomb.

[22] '*Philosophical Bibliotheca*'

[23] Axiomata

[24] 'Rota Mundi'

[25] Proteus – A Greek God of the Sea; a servant of Poseidon and 'shepherd' of seals. He possessed the power of prophecy.

CHAPTER FIVE

Chapter Five

The Tomb

Now, the true and original story of our discovery of the greatly enlightened man of God, Brother C.R.C., is this:

After A. died in Gallia Narbonensi[26], he was succeeded by our beloved Brother N.N. after he had come to us and taken the solemn oath of fidelity and secrecy.

He told us in confidence that A. had comforted him by saying that this Brotherhood would not remain hidden for much longer but would soon be admirable, helpful and essential to the whole German nation.

The year after he had fulfilled his studies, he was of the mind to move on, having been provided with sufficient funds to do so. Being a good Architect, he planned to improve part of his building. As part of the renovations he concentrated on the memorial plaque, which was cast of brass and contained the names of all who had belonged to the Brotherhood. He decided to transfer this, together with a few other items he had found, into a more fitting vault. As, where or when Brother Ch.[27] died or in which country he was buried, was unknown to us, having been kept secret by our predecessors.

The panel was held firmly by a large, strong nail. It was drawn out with some force and took a large chunk of what first seemed like ordinary stone with it. This revealed the thin wall to be plaster, which had been concealing a hidden door. With joyful anticipation, we took down the rest of the wall and cleared it away from the door. Written upon the door in great letters was a year and, above that, the phrase 'After 120 years I shall open' [28]. We gave thanks to God and decided to leave it overnight so that we would not neglect the duties on our rota.

Referring again to our *'Confession'*; what we are writing here is done for the good of the worthy. The unworthy, God willing, will see little benefit from it. For, just as our door was miraculously revealed after so many years; a door to Europe (when its own wall is removed) will also be revealed. This is already partly appearing and is greatly desired by many.

The next morning we opened the door. A vault appeared before our eyes with seven sides and seven corners. Each side was eight feet high and five feet wide. Although the vault was completely shut off from daylight, it was nevertheless lit by another 'sun', which had drawn its light from the Sun and was situated in the upper part of the centre of the ceiling. In the middle, instead of a tombstone, was a round Altar covered with a plate of brass.

Engraved upon the plate was this:

A.C.R.C.[29] *'Unto the glory of the Rose and Cross, I have, in my lifetime, made this compendium of the universe as my tomb'*[30].

Around the first circle or edge was written:
JESUS, my all [31].

In the middle were four figures, enclosed in a circle, on which was written:
1. *There is no empty space*[32]
2. *The Yoke of Law*[33]
3. *Gospel of Freedom*[34]
4. *The whole glory of God*[35]

This was all clear and bright, as were the seven sides and the two heptagons; so we all knelt together and gave thanks to the only wise, only mighty and only eternal God, who has taught us more than all men's wits could have learned; Praised be His holy name.

The vault was composed of three sections; the upper part or ceiling, the wall or sides and the ground or floor.

All we shall say about the upper part for now is that it was divided into triangles, with the seven sides around the bright centre.

But as for what is inside; you who would wish to join us shall, God Willing, see it with your own eyes.

Every side or wall is divided into ten squares, each one containing several figures and words which are clearly and faithfully shown in our book 'Concentrate'[36].

The floor was also divided into triangles but, because it describes the power and rule of the Devil, we will not go into detail in case the information is abused by the evil and ungodly world.

But those that have a heavenly antidote may tread upon and bruise the head of the old and evil serpent without fear or injury - which is appropriate for our time.

Every side or wall had a door which opened to a chest[37]. Within these chests were a variety of objects, most notably all of our books, which we already owned, with the exception of the *'Dictionary of Theophrastus Paracelsus von Hohenheim'* [38] and those we use on a daily basis. Within, we also found his travel itinerary and biography, which we have used to tell this story.

In another chest were mirrors of various quality and elsewhere were little bells, burning lamps and wonderful, glorious, musical chants. It was all constructed so that, even if hundreds of years should pass and the Order or Brotherhood was no more, it could be completely restored upon the discovery of this single archive.

We had not yet seen the dead body of our careful and wise founder, so we moved the altar to one side. This allowed us access to a heavy brass plate, which we lifted and found a corpse, uncorrupted and whole, as if alive, with fine regalia and accessories. In his hand he held a book written in Gold on parchment titled 'T.'[39] which, after the Bible is now our greatest treasure and should not lightly be subjected to the judgement of the world[40]. At the end of the book, this verse is written:

A seed planted in the breast of Jesus[41]

Ch. Ros. C. was descended from the noble and respectable German R.C. family. He had through divine revelations and astute conclusions, together with his own tireless effort, gained access to the heavenly and earthly mysteries or secrets.

During his travels in Arabia and Africa he gathered more than the wealth that was contained in any royal or imperial treasury. For all that, his time had not yet come but this should be kept secret until later times.

He divided all this together with his own knowledge so that the faithful and sworn successors could be educated.

He also made a model of the earth, completely consistent with the known facts in every way and was also eventually able to write an outline of a story of past, present and future events.

He lived more than one hundred years. Although he was quite frail, he did not suffer illness or disease but invoked God and, surrounded by his brothers, returned his enlightened soul to his faithful Creator.

He was, above all, our revered Founder, our fascinating Brother, the most faithful teacher, the reliable friend and has now been hidden from us in his secret resting place during the 120 years since his death.[42]

Underneath they had recorded their names:
1. Brother I.A. - elected by Brother Ch.[43] as head of the Brotherhood
2. Brother G.V.M.P.G.[44]
3. Brother R.C. - Junior heir of the Holy Spirit
4. Brother F.B.M.P.A. - Painter and architect [45]
5. Brother G.G.M.P.I. - Cabalist

Second Circle

1. Brother P.A. Successor, Brother I.O. Mathematician.
2. Brother A. Successor, Brother P.D.
3. Brother R. Successor of father Ch.R.C. triumphant with Christ.[46]

At the end was written :

'We are born of God,

We die in Jesus,

We come to life again through the holy spirit' [47]

At that time, Brother I.O and Brother P.D [48] were dead but where are *they* buried?

Doubtless, our Senior Brothers were also buried in a similar and special manner, possibly hidden in the same way: We hope that our example will encourage others to research the other names (which is why we have published them) and search for the places of their burial. Most of them, because of their practices and healing are still known and praised amongst the elderly. Perhaps this is how we may increase our treasures?[49] Or at least clear up a few matters.

Concerning *'The Concise Universe'*[50] or 'microcosm'; we found it had been kept in another little altar, more exquisite than you could possibly imagine but we shall not go into detail until asked by our true hearted Brothers.

And so, we have covered it again with the plates, replaced the altar on top, shut the door and secured it with all our seals.

Besides this, in the course of our duties, some more books have come to light, amongst them 'M.' (these were published by the commendable M.P. despite his many other responsibilities).

Finally, we went our separate ways and left our jewels to the natural heirs. Now, we await the comments and critique of scholars and uneducated alike.

CHAPTER FIVE: NOTES

[26] *'Gaul of Narbonne'* - A Roman Province located in what is now Languedoc and Provence.

[27] The original German says 'Fr Ch' at this point whereas all other versions have 'RC'.

[28] The Latin inscription above the door; *'Post 120 annos patebo'* is usually stated to be 'After 120 years I shall open' or 'After 120 years I will open'.

[29] Sometimes given as A.G.R.C. (*Ad Glorium Rosae Cruicis*) which means 'to the glory of the Rosy Cross'. However, it is clearly A.C.R.C. in the original text. It is therefore likely that it is 'something-beginning-with-A' Christian Rosencreutz – possibly 'Adeptus' (Adept) or 'Architectus' (Architect).

[30] Hoc universi compendium unius mihi sepulchrum feci

[31] This is usually written as 'Jesus mihi omnia' but the original German writes 'Jesus' as 'IESVS' in capitals.

[32] Nequaquam vacuum

[33] Legis Jugum

[34] Libertas Evangelij

[35] Dei gloria intacta

[36] *'Concentratum'*

[37] Vaughan translates this as 'chest' but many other versions use 'cabinet' or 'closet' which seems to make more sense. The original German uses the word 'Kasten' here, which is 'a box'. Although it can be used to describe a cabinet, it would be more usual to use the word 'Schrank' so, in this case, I will stick with Vaughan's translation.

[38] 'Vocabular of Theoph: Par. Ho.' is usually written here but the original German is not abbreviated and reads: 'Vocabulario Theophrasti Paracelsi ab Hohenheim'. It is also worth noting that the Brothers 'finding books which we already had, with the exception of…' could be read to suggest that they did not have the 'Vocabular' but found it in the tomb. However, as Paracelsus was born in 1493 and the death of CRC would have been 1484, then it means that CRC could not have been entombed for 120 years with this work by Paracelsus; thus meaning that 'with the exception of' implies that the Brothers owned this work but <u>did not</u> find it in the tomb.

[39] Vaughan has 'I' as the name of the book. The Original German says T for the book and this is often interpreted as meaning 'Testament'.

[40] Vaughan puts that it *ought to be* delivered to the censure of the World, which is the precise opposite meaning of the German text.

[41] The Latin reads 'Granum pectori Iesu insitum'

[42] The full passage in Latin is:
'Ch. Ros. C. ex nobili atque splendida Germaniae R.C. familia oriundus, vir sui seculi divinis revelationibus subtilissimis imaginationibus, indefessis laboribus ad coelestia, atque humana mysteria ; arcanave admissus postquam suam (quam Arabico, & Africano itineribus Collegerat) plusquam regiam, atque imperatoriam Gazam suo seculo nondum convenientem, posteritati eruendam custo divisset et jam suarum Artium, ut et nominis, fides acconjunctissimos herides instituisset, mundum minutum omnibus motibus magno illi respondentem fabricasset hocque tandem preteritarum, praesentium, et futurarum, rerum compendio extracto, centenario major non morbo (quem ipse nunquam corpore expertus erat, nunquam alios infestare sinebat) ullo pellente sed spiritu Dei evocante, illuminatam animam (inter Fratrum amplexus et ultima oscula) fidelissimo creatori Deo reddidisset, Pater dilectissimus, Fra: suavissimus, praeceptor fidelissimus amicus integerimus, a suis ad 120 annos hic absconditus est.'

[43] Usually given as 'C.R.' but Vaughan has C.H. It is 'Ch' in the German.

[44] Vaughan writes this as GVMPC; it is actually GVMPG

[45] 'Brother B.M., - Painter and architect for P.A.' is the usual translation in English versions and is given by Vaughan as 'Fra: B.M. P.A.' but the original German printing is clearly in the form of: 'Fr.F.B.M.P.A. painter and architect'.

[46] English (Vaughan) again says C.R.C but original German is Ch.R.C.

[47] 'Ex Deo Nascimur, in Jesu morimur, per spiritum sanctum reviviscimus'

[48] I.O. and D is given in English – original German is IO and PD.

[49] 'Gaza' is given here which has been substituted with 'treasure' whenever it is used. This use is of Persian origin and the English New Testament translates the word 'Gaza' as treasure in Acts 8:27 and 'Treasury' in Mark 12:41-43, Luke 21:1 and John 8:20.

[50] 'Minitum Mundum'

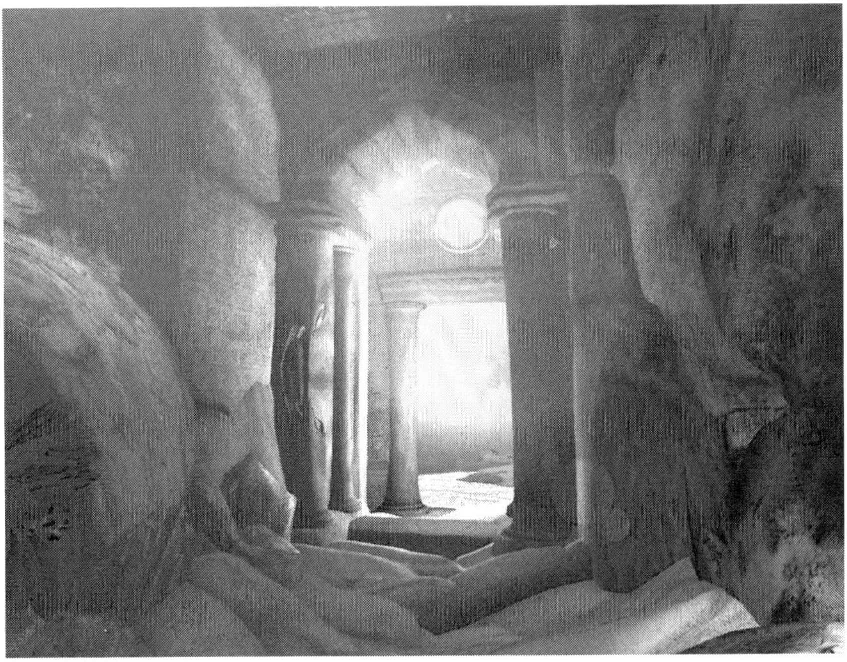

Chapter Six

To a New Brotherhood

Now we know that a reformation of the divine and the mundane will soon come, as we desire and others anticipate. For it is fitting that, before the rising of the Sun, Aurora (a divine light or a bright clarity) should appear and break out in the sky.

So, in the meantime, the few who will put their names forward, may join together to increase the numbers and prestige of our Brotherhood. To happily make a start on the philosophical principles given to us by our Brother C. To humbly and with love take part with us in exploring our treasures (which cannot fail or be wasted), until the labours of this world are taken from us. And to not be so blind to the knowledge of the wonderful works of God.

But, so that every Christian may know what religion and beliefs we have, we are committed to have the knowledge of Jesus Christ and profess that it is most clear and pure, the same as is practised nowadays, especially in Germany. Free from all fanatics, heretics and false prophets who are maintained, defended and encouraged in certain other countries.

Also, we use two sacraments as they have been established in accordance with the procedures and ceremonies of the first reformed Church.

In political terms, we recognise the Roman Empire as our state and the Fourth Kingdom[51] as our Christian ruler. We know there will be changes and would willingly communicate the same, with all our hearts, to other godly and educated men. Despite this, the writing is in our hands and no one, save God alone, can make it common knowledge and no unworthy person is able to take it from us.

But we shall secretly help this good cause, as God shall allow or prevent us. For our gold is not blind like the Heathen's Fate, but is the Church's ornament and to the honour of the Temple.

Also, our philosophy is not a new invention. It was received by Adam after his fall and was used by Moses and Solomon. She should not be doubted or contradicted by other opinions or meanings. The truth is harmonious, brief and consistent and in keeping with Jesus in every way, as he is the true image of his father and is therefore His likeness.

It will not be said that 'This is true according to philosophy but untrue according to theology' but rather where Plato, Aristotle, Pythagoras and others got it right and where Enoch, Abraham, Moses, Solomon were concerned; it all comes down to the same thing. Especially where it all coincides with that wonderful book, The Bible.

All of this is in agreement and forms a sphere or globe, whose parts are all equidistant from the centre. In accordance with this, what is in that centre will be discussed and explained clearly and fully in Christian parables.

But now (as it is the popular subject at this time), let us turn to the dreaded 'Goldmaking' which seems to have gained the upper hand. So much so that, under its banner, many crooks and conmen operate criminally; deceiving, robbing and taking credit which is not due to them.

Yes, nowadays, even intelligent men still consider the transmutation of metals to be the pinnacle of philosophy. It is their sole purpose and ultimate desire, thinking that God would feel respected and honoured by them. In making great quantities of gold and spontaneous prayers they hope to reach God, who knows all and searches every heart.

Therefore, we publicly state that the true philosophers are of another opinion entirely – thinking little of the making of gold, which is just a minor matter. They have a thousand better things they can be doing.

And we say with our loving founder C.R.C.[52] 'Hah! Gold isn't that much in itself!' as to them the whole of nature is revealed.

He does not rejoice just because he can make gold or, as Christ says, 'the Devils are under his command'. He rejoices because he sees the heavens open up and sees the angels of God ascending and descending and to have his name written in the book of life.

Also, we will testify that many books and pictures produced under the name of alchemy are an insult to God's glory. We will name them in due course and will give a list of them to the pure of heart.

And we ask that all scholars watch out for these kinds of books; for the enemy never rests but instead plants his weeds until something stronger uproots him.

So, according to the intent and wishes of Brother C.R.C., we his Brothers, once again ask all scholars of Europe this:

That all who read our *Fama* (which we have produced in five languages) and *Confession*, to please carefully consider our offer.

To scrutinise and test their arts right now, and to publish their thoughts either individually or as a group.

And, although we have not yet given our names or meetings, rest assured that everyone's opinions will find their way to us, in whatever language. Nor will anyone who tries to make contact, either by word of mouth or by writing, and wishes to speak with us, be ignored.

And, this is a promise: That anyone who genuinely, from his heart, reaches out to us will be rewarded in goods, body and soul but he who is false or only after money will not be able to harm us in any manner but will instead be brought to utter ruin and destruction.

Also, our building (even if seen by almost one hundred thousand people) will forever remain, untouched, intact and hidden from the godless world

Under the shadow of thy wings, oh Lord.[53]

CHAPTER SIX: NOTES

[51] The 'Fourth Kingdom' or 'Fourth Monarchy'. Adolf Santing in his book '*De Manifesten der Rozenkruisers*' claimed that it comprised Germany, Sicily, Lombardy and Burgundy. However, it seems more likely that this is a reference to the Fourth Kingdom in the Bible, prophesised in the book of Daniel to be the precursor to the End Times. It was widely used in the Protestant Reformation in the 16th Century as the 'Universal History' of the world. The kingdoms are usually interpreted as; The Babylonian Empire, The Persian Empire, The Greek Empire (Alexander the Great) and The Roman Empire. There are many other interpretations but the significance is that after the End Times, will come the final kingdom which is The Kingdom of God.

[52] RCC in English, CRC in original German)

[53] Latin is '*Sub umbra Alarum tuarum Jehovah*'

Confessio Fraternitatis

PREFACE

Preface

Dear Reader,

Here you will find our Confession which gives thirty seven reasons for our purpose and intentions. You may, at your leisure, investigate and analyse them and consider if they are of interest to you.

It takes great effort to convince people of things that are yet to come but when everything is finally revealed in the full light of day, we will probably all be ashamed that we ever questioned them.

With the same conviction that we use to call the Pope the Antichrist (which was a capital offence in the past), we know with certainty that what we keep secret now will thunder forth with an uplifted voice in the future.

We wish with all our hearts that this day will be soon.

Brothers of R.C.

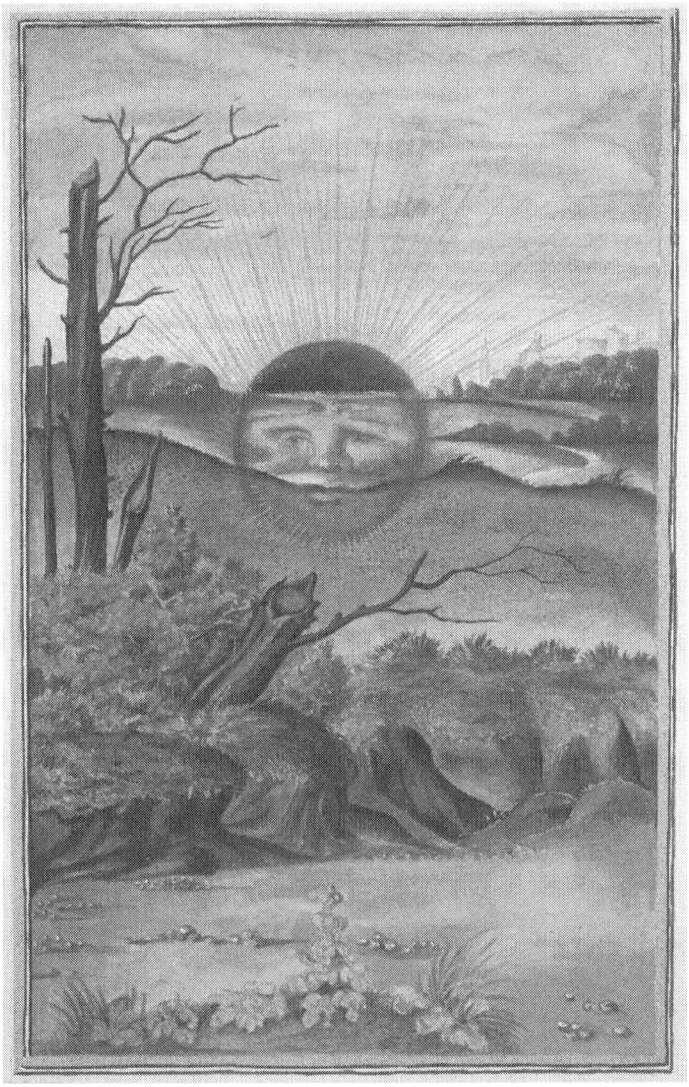

Chapter One

Confessio Fraternitatis or The Confession of the Laudable Fraternity of the Most Honourable Order of the Rosy Cross

To all the scholars of Europe,

What is published and reported concerning our Brotherhood and contained within the Fama, is not a mere work of fiction. It should be taken seriously and not regarded as a metaphor.

It is the Lord Jehovah who is changing the course of nature. The Lord's Sabbath is coming soon and the first part of his plan is almost completed.

And what has previously taken great and daily effort to discover is now made apparent to even the most casual seeker. Although it is forced on them in a way, in order to ease the workload of the godly and so it is no longer subject to good or bad luck. But the wickedness of the ungodly will still get its deserved punishment.

Although we cannot be accused of heresy, scheming or political motives, we criticize both East and West (by which we mean the Pope and Mohammed) as blasphemers against our Lord Jesus Christ. With goodwill we offer our prayers, secrets and great treasures of gold to the head of the Roman Empire.

For the sake of academic standards we feel that this should be expanded upon and a better explanation given, in case there is anything that is too deep, obscure or unclear within the Fama or has been omitted for certain reasons. We hope by this that scholars will be much more interested and inclined to our purpose.

Chapter Two

Concerning the alteration and amendment of philosophy, we have already clearly stated that this subject is weak and faulty. We know that most people falsely claim that it is stable and strong (goodness knows how!) but all the same, it is clearly on its way out.

But, in the same way that, in a place or country where there is an outbreak of a new disease, nature also provides a cure within the same place; so a remedy for the many weaknesses of philosophy appears.

This is given to our native country so philosophy may become stable again, renewed and refreshed.

We have no other philosophy other than that which is the complete content of all faculties, sciences and arts. It contains much of theology and medicine but little about the wisdom of the law and persistently searches heaven and earth. Or, to briefly mention it, all scholars who make themselves known to us and join our brotherhood will learn more wonderful secrets than they ever believed possible or thought were achievable.

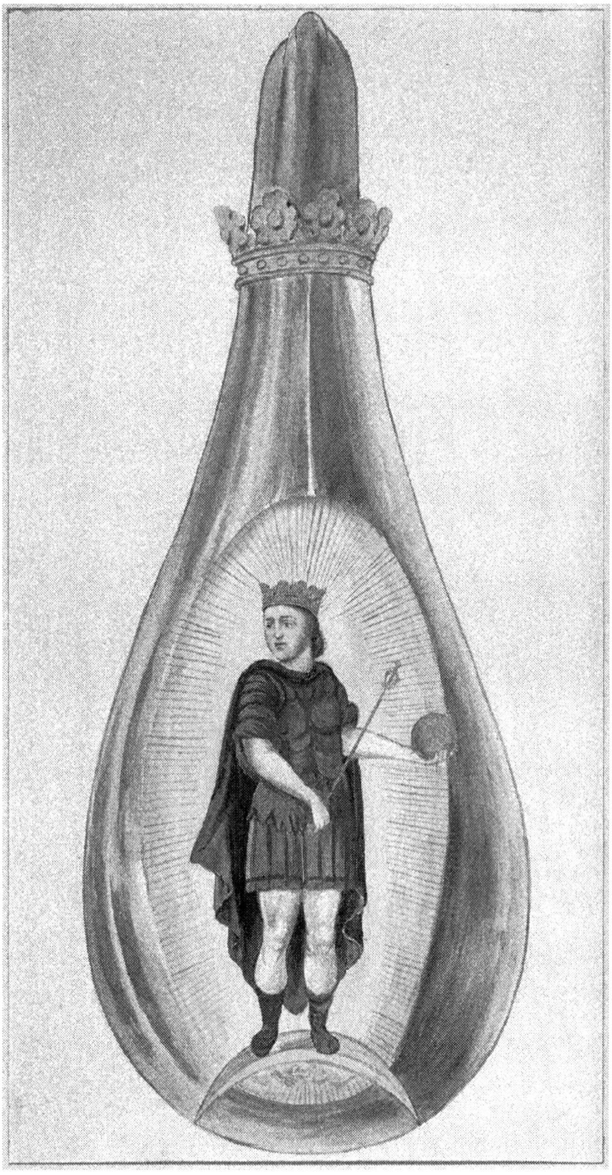

Chapter Three

To briefly state what we mean, we need to proceed carefully so that there will not only be an interest in meeting us and gaining our advice but that everyone will know that, although we do not take such mysteries and secrets lightly, we consider it right and proper that this knowledge should be revealed to many.

For it is to be taught and believed, that our willing offer will initiate a variety of conflicting thoughts in men, who are entering an, as yet unknown, sixth age (a *'Miranda sexta aetatis'*). Otherwise, those who look to the future are preoccupied by current events, so that they live in the world like blind fools, who on a sunny day cannot see the bright sun and know nothing but the feeling of it.

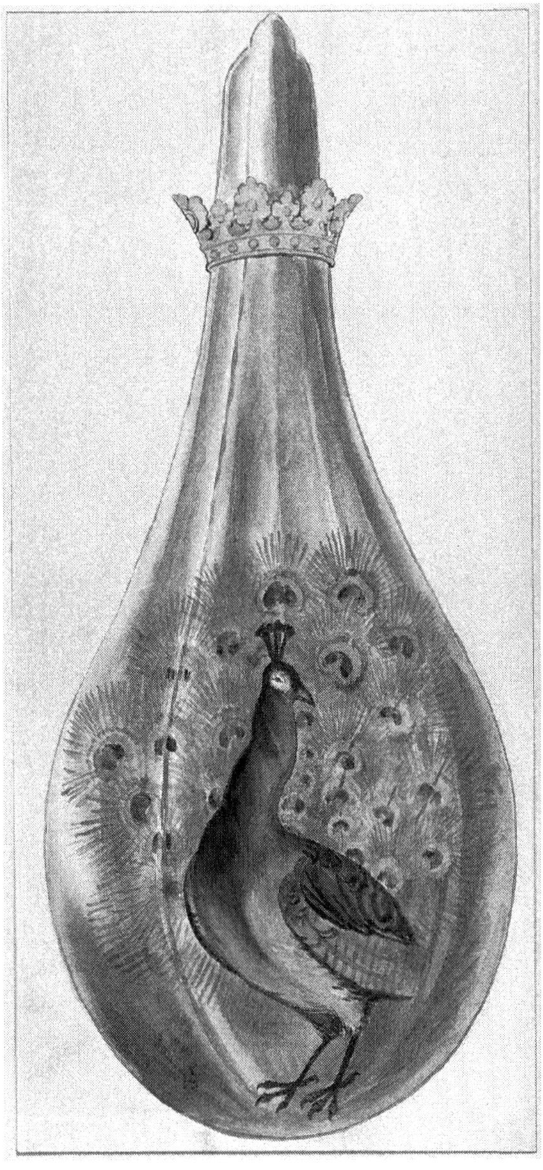

Chapter Four

Concerning the first part, we believe that the meditations, inquiries and inventions of our beloved father Christian[54] are the most excellent, great and glorious. For, from the beginning of the world until now, the human mind has discovered, invented, produced, corrected and disseminated knowledge. Whether from divine revelation, through the service of the angels and spirits, from sharpness and depth of understanding, or through experimentation, observation and experience.

If God saw fit to destroy all other books so that all other writings and learnings should be lost, even then the future generations will still be able to lay a new foundation, and bring the truth to light again from the works of our father Christian alone.

This new beginning would be quite easy if one begins to pull down and destroy the old ruined building, and then to enlarge the porch, fit new lights into the rooms, and then change the doors, stairs, and other things according to our will.

Who would object to this – to display it to everyone rather than keep it locked away like some special ornament for a future occasion?

For what reason should we not stay with the one truth (which many men seek through crooked streets and wrong turns) with all our hearts, if it pleases God to light the sixth candle?

Wouldn't it be good to not have to care; to not fear hunger, poverty, sickness and age?

Wouldn't it be so precious if you could always live like this, as if you had been alive from the beginning of the world and carry on living like this until the end?

Wouldn't it be nice to live in one place and not even people living beyond the River Ganges in India or as far away as Peru could hide anything or keep their information secret from you?

Wouldn't it be good to read only one book and after having read only that book you would understand and remember everything that could be learned from all other books, past, present or future?

How pleasant it would be if you could sing and, instead of pebbles, you could attract pearls and jewels. Instead of wild animals you attract the spirits and instead of the Devil[55], captivate the powerful, the mighty princes of the world.

Oh people, God's plan is quite different. He has now decided to increase the number of our brotherhood. We have undertaken this with much joy as until now, we have received these great treasures without merit. Yes, regardless of our hopes, thoughts and purpose.

And with a similar joy we are now devoted to put it into practice. Not even the compassion and pity for our own children (which some of us in the Brotherhood do have), will distract us from it because we know these unexpected goods cannot be inherited or obtained by luck.

CHAPTER FOUR: NOTES

[54] English translations say 'Christian Father' whereas the Latin and German takes the form 'father Christian'.

[55] I have used Devil here, as it is more familiar. The Latin version uses Pluto (the ruler of the Underworld).

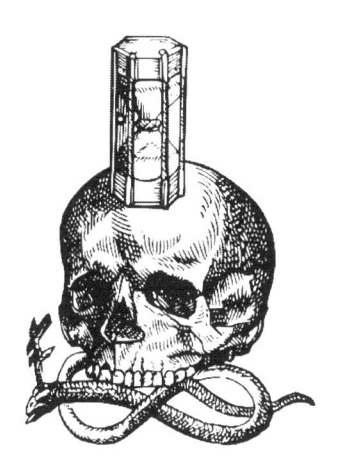

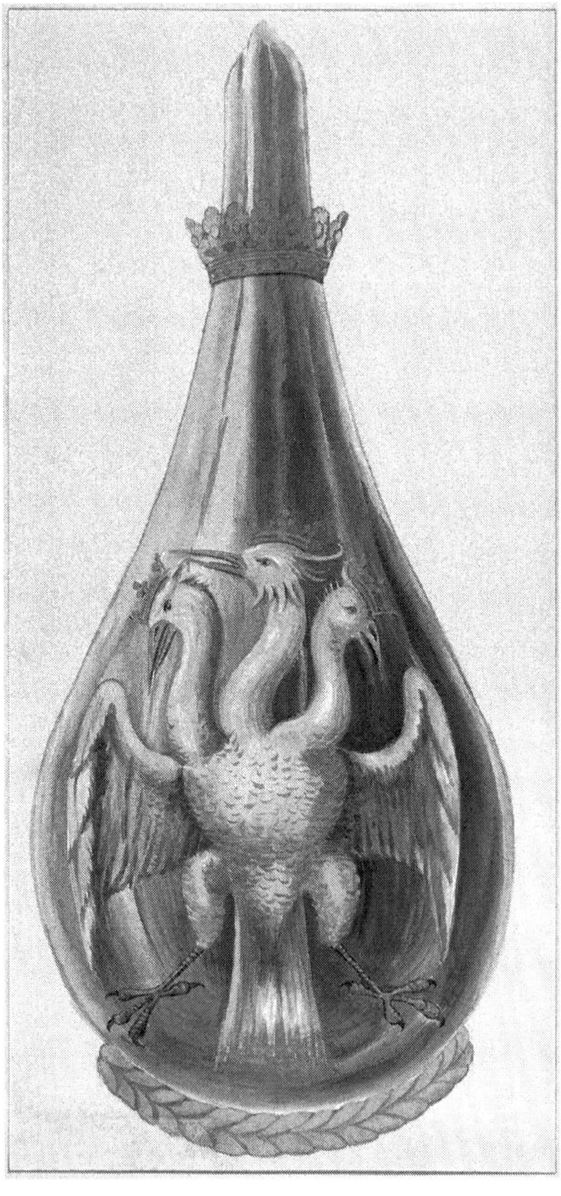

Chapter Five

If there is anybody who wants to complain about our judgement - that we offer our treasure so freely and fully to all men without making distinctions between pious men, scholars, the wise, royalty and the common people – then we will not contradict them. That is too flippant and easy to do. But, we will say this much; that our *Arcana* or secrets will not be made public.

Although the Fama has been published in five languages and is available to everyone, we are well aware that the uneducated and ignorant will not understand nor appreciate it. Also, the worthiness of those accepted into our Brotherhood is not done so by man's judgement and caution but by the rule of our revelation and manifestation.

Because of this, the unworthy can call out and shout a thousand times. They can present themselves and apply to us a thousand times. God has commanded that our ears shall hear none of it. Yes, God has protected us with his clouds that no violence or force can be committed against us, his servants. As a result, we cannot be seen or discovered by anyone, unless he has the eyes of an eagle.

It has been necessary to publish the Fama in everyone's mother tongue so those that God has not excluded from the happiness of this

Brotherhood should not be deprived of its knowledge, even though they are uneducated.

The Brotherhood will be divided into certain separate degrees in a similar way that those who live in the city of Damcar[56] in Arabia have a different political structure to other Arabians. Only wise and understanding men govern there and, with the king's permission, make specific laws.

In this manner, this type of government shall be established in Europe after the first phase is complete and in preparation for the next phase (our Christianly Father has laid out details of this).

And from then, our trumpet shall sound loudly and openly. It will be announced freely and publicly. The whole world shall hear of what is now only represented in secret pictures and diagrams and shown to only a few.

In this manner, many godly people have secretly and desperately pushed against the Pope's tyranny in the past. As a result of this and with great enthusiasm, he was thrown from his seat by Germany and trampled underfoot. His final fall is yet to come and is earmarked for our times, when he shall be clawed apart and his ass's cry shall come to an end, replaced by a new voice.

We know that this is already apparent to many scholars in Germany as their writings and secret celebrations clearly suggest.

CHAPTER FIVE: NOTES

[56] The Latin uses 'Damcar' rather than 'Damascum' (Damascus). I have therefore kept to the convention I previously applied in the Fama and taken Damcar as a different place to Damascus.

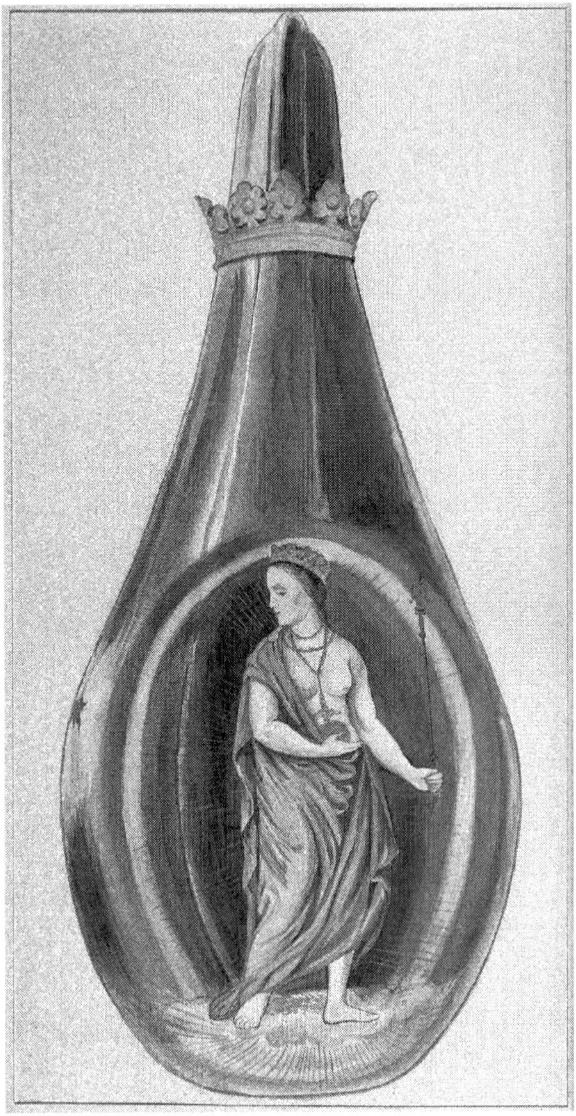

Chapter Six

Here we could write everything that has happened from the year of Our Lord 1378 (in which year our Christian Father was born) until now and recount the changes he saw in his one hundred and six years of life and which, after his death, he has passed down to our Brethren and our successors.

But we must be brief, which does not allow us to give a full account of it until a more fitting time. For now, it is enough that those who do not despise our declaration so far, prepare the path for our acquaintance and friendship.

Yet, he whom the Lord God has allowed to see, understand and use those great letters and characters that have been written and imprinted in heaven and earth's structure for his instruction. And which He has renewed for us throughout all changes of government that have occurred from time to time. This man, although he does not realize it yet, is already our friend.

And as we know he will not resent our invitation and so that there is no cause to fear deception, we promise and state openly that no one who makes himself known to us under the seal of secrecy and desires our Brotherhood shall be misled by his own honesty and hopefulness.

But, to the false hypocrites and those seeking anything other than wisdom: we state here and now that we cannot be revealed to you or betrayed. And without the will of God you will be unable to cause any harm but you will certainly receive the punishment spoken of in our Fama.

So their evil plans will rebound upon them and our treasures shall remain untouched and unaffected until the Lion comes, when he will request them for his own use and apply them to support and establish his kingdom.

Chapter Seven

We should here clearly state and make it known to everyone that God has definitely and confidently decided to send a gift to the world before her end. This will be such a truth, light, life and glory as the first man Adam had in paradise before it was lost by him and he and his descendants were driven to misery.

As a result, all servitude, falsehood, lies, and darkness (which, with the spinning of the world, has little by little crept into all arts, works, and governments of men, and has darkened most parts of them), will cease.

For from there sprang all number of false opinions and heresies so that even the wisest was not able to know whose beliefs and opinions he should follow and accept, as they could not easily be distinguished from one another. On the one hand, there was the Fama of the philosophers, whilst on the other hand there was their true experience of them.

Of all this, when it is abolished and removed and a right and true rule instituted in its place, all that shall remain is gratitude to those who have contributed. But the work itself shall be attributed to the blessedness of our age.

We now openly confess that, although the writings of notable men will greatly advance this coming reformation, we do not wish to be credited with this honour ourselves. This would make it seem as if the work was just a task we had been given and told to do.

But we confess, and state openly in the name of the Lord Jesus Christ that even the stones shall arise and offer their services before there is any lack of workers to accomplish God's plan.

Chapter Eight

Indeed, the Lord God has already sent certain messengers as evidence of his will. Namely, some new stars which have appeared in the sky and can be observed in the constellations of Ophiuchus (*Serpentario or Serpent*) and Cygnus (*Cygno or Swan*). They appear to everyone as powerful signs of hugely significant matters.

The secrets of his writings and characters are essential so that man may discover all of these things. But, although the great book of nature is open to all men, there are very few who can read and understand it. Because, just as man is given two organs to hear with, two to see, two to smell but only one to speak; it would be hopeless to expect the ears to speak or the eyes to hear. And so, there have been ages or times which have seen and others which have heard or smelt.

And now, very soon, this honour shall be given to the tongue and what has in past times been seen, heard and smelt shall finally be spoken. The World shall awaken from her heavy, drunken sleep caused by the poisoned cup and with an open heart, bareheaded and barefooted, will merrily and joyfully greet the new rising Sun.

CHAPTER NINE

Chapter Nine

These characters and letters which have, here and there, been incorporated in the Holy Scriptures we call the Bible, have also been imprinted on the creations of heaven and earth and upon all animals. So that, just as a mathematician and astronomer can calculate when an eclipse will occur, so we may know and predict when the period of darkness that obscures the Church will end.

We have derived our magical writing from these characters or letters. Moreover, we have discovered and constructed a new language for ourselves with which we are able to describe the nature of all things.

So it is little wonder that we are not quite as eloquent in other languages. These, we know, are different from the language of our forefathers Adam and Enoch, which was completely hidden by the Babylonical confusion.

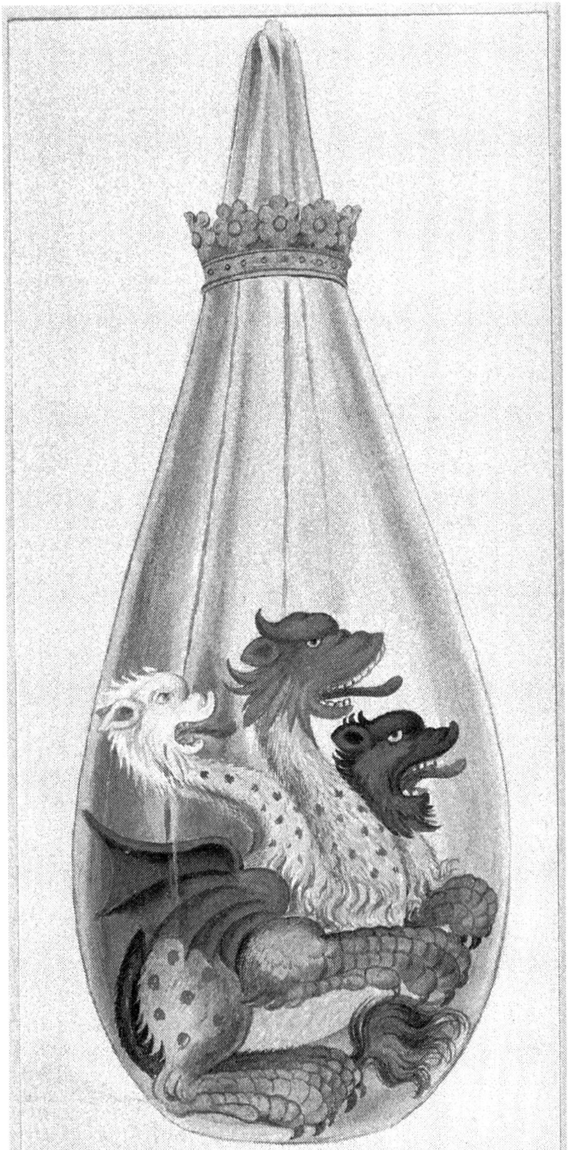

Chapter Ten

But you must also understand that there are still some eagles' feathers in our way which hinder our purpose. Because of this we recommend that everyone should continue to read the Holy Bible diligently. As those who derive their joy from this should know that they are preparing an excellent way by which they may come to our Brotherhood.

For this is the entirety of our regulations - that every letter or character that is found in the world ought to be observed and learned well.

So, those who are like us and are close to us and who make the Holy Bible the rule of their life and the ultimate goal of their studies, let this be the summary and contents of the whole world. Not only to have it always upon the lips but to know how to apply and direct the true understanding of it to all times and ages of the world.

Also, it is not our way to compromise and debase the Holy Scriptures. For there are plenty who do; some misleading and twisting it for their own ends, some scandalizing it and wickedly falsifying. All of which suits the clerics, philosophers, physicians, and mathematicians. Against all of this, we openly proclaim that, since the beginning of the world, man has never been given a more worthy, admirable and wholesome book than the Holy Bible.

Blessed is he that has it, more blessed is he who reads it diligently, but most blessed of all is he who truly understands it, for he is closest to God.

Chapter Eleven

Regardless of what has been said in the Fama concerning our contempt for the fraudulent alchemists and the transmutation of metals, and of the highest medicine in the world, this should be understood: we do not discount or have any contempt for this great gift of God. Not just because it brings the knowledge of nature and medicine but because it reveals countless secrets and wonders to us.

It is therefore required that we must be determined to achieve an understanding and knowledge of philosophy.

Furthermore, sharp minds should not be distracted by the shine of metals before they are familiar with the knowledge of nature.

To come this far, he needs to be an insatiable creature; he who will not be deterred by poverty or sickness. However, he who is raised above all men and gains control over all that troubles other men or causes them anguish and pain, will instead apply himself to more trivial matters such as building houses, waging wars and taking pride in himself, as he has an infinite store of gold and silver.

God does not like this, for he elevates the lowly and knocks down the proud with contempt. He sends his holy angel to speak with those with modest achievements but he forces the loud and obnoxious alone into the wilderness.

This is the rightful reward for the Roman imposters, who have spewed out blasphemies against Christ and continue with their lies even in this clear shining light.

In Germany, all of their crimes and despicable tricks have been exposed and the extent of their sins fully measured so that their entire punishment may be decided. Therefore, in the future, the mouths of these vipers will be shut and the triple crown[57] rendered powerless, as we will clearly detail when we meet you.

CHAPTER ELEVEN: NOTES

[57] This is often translated as 'Triple Horn' rather than triple crown. It has probably been adjusted in order to link to the Biblical Daniel and the Antichrist prophecy, where a little horn first uproots three of ten horns. It has been interpreted as the fall of the Heruli, Vandals and Ostrogoths, which were three of ten Western divisions of Rome. The power of the little horn has been referred to the Papacy and therefore ties in with '*With the same conviction that we use to call the Pope the Antichrist*' seen in the Preface. However, the Latin gives this as 'Corona triplex' so I have stuck with 'Triple Crown'

Chapter Twelve

In conclusion, we urge you to put away most, if not all, of the books written by false alchemists. Such as those who think it is a trivial matter or some kind of joke to misuse the Holy Trinity or apply it inappropriately to nonsense. Or those who use mysterious and impenetrable language and diagrams to deliberately confuse and deceive people, and con the foolish for their money. Nowadays, there are far too many of these books being published, foremost amongst them the stadium comedian[58] who is a clever impostor. The enemy of man's welfare deliberately mixes these with the good publications, which makes the truth hard to determine. Truth is, in itself, simple, clear and easy to understand. Lies, on the other hand, are loud, brash and polished brightly so they have the appearance of divine or human wisdom.

You who are wise, turn your back on books like this and turn instead to us. We are not after your money but willingly offer you our great treasures instead. We do not want to take your wealth by selling fake medicines but, on the contrary, wish you to sample some of *our* goods.

We talk to you, not using parables, but are happy and willing to show you a correct, simple, full explanation and knowledge of all secrets.

We do not ask to be received by you but instead invite you to our more than royal houses and palaces. This invitation is not sent by our own initiative but, as you should know, because we are compelled by the spirit of God to do so and because of the significance of this present time.

CHAPTER TWELVE: NOTES

[58] The description is 'Amphitheatral Comedian': possibly Heinrich Khunrath, the author of '*Amphitheatrum Sapientiae Aeternae* (The Amphitheatre of Eternal Wisdom)' who died in 1605. He was a devotee of Paracelsus and praised John Dee in his writings. He is considered a direct link between John Dee and the Rosicrucianism that followed the publication of the Fama. If it is he, quite what he might have done to be referred to as a 'comedian' is unclear.

Chapter Thirteen

Loving people, what do you think? How has this affected you, now that you understand and realise that we truly and sincerely give our allegiance to Christ, condemn the Pope, devote ourselves to the true philosophy, lead a life worthy of a man and invite and accept many others who have seen the same light of God into our Brotherhood every day?

Consider now how you might make a start with us. Not only by meditating on the gifts that you possess and your personal experience of God. But carefully consider the imperfections in all arts and other things that currently do not make sense and seek to amend them. Also, to attempt to satisfy God and fully prepare yourself for the empire of the time in which you are living.

If you do this, you will be rewarded in this way: all things of nature throughout the world shall be collected and given to you, as in the centre of the sun and moon. You will be free of all that obscures man's understanding and impedes progress, like all the eccentric circles and epicycles.

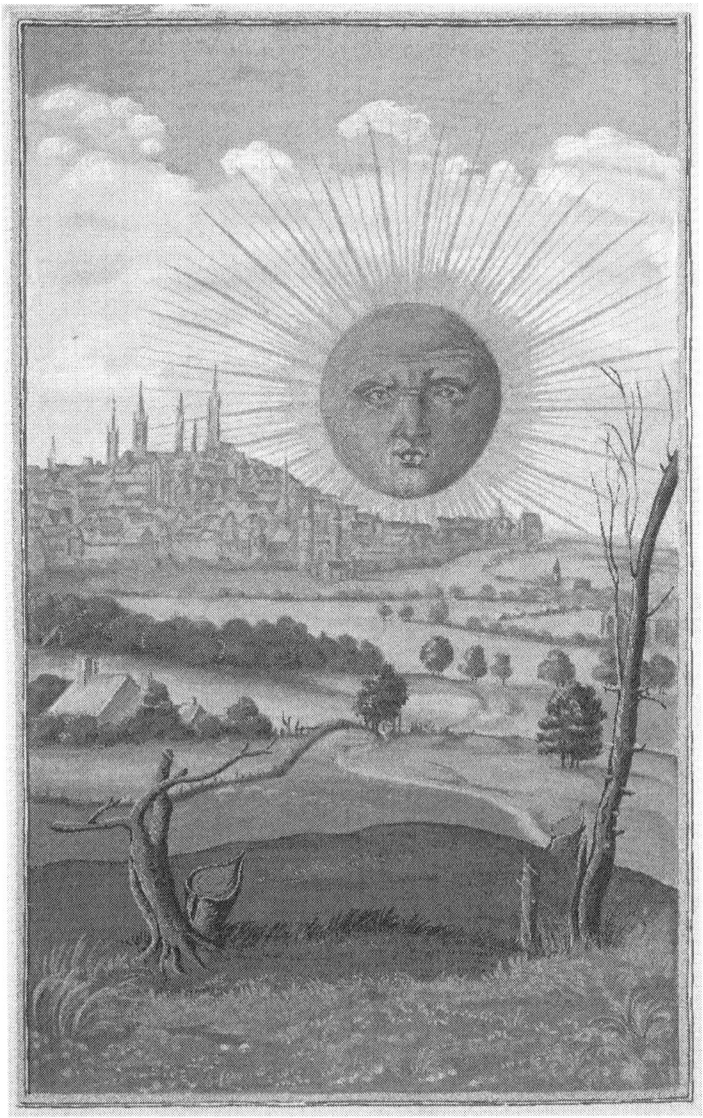

Chapter Fourteen

But those practical and curious men, who are either blinded by the glittering of gold or (to tell the truth) are honest at the moment but think such great riches will never fail them. They may easily be corrupted, become idle or fall into a hedonistic lifestyle.

Those men, we hope, will not disturb our sacred silence with their noise.

Let them think that they can get a medicine that fully cures all diseases. It does not matter. Those whom God has decided to strike down with such diseases and whom he wishes to keep in line will never be able to get such a medicine.

In this way, even though we might enrich the whole world, provide it with learning and release it from suffering, we shall never be revealed to everyone unless with God's special approval.

Whoever wishes to benefit from and partake of our riches without the approval of God, will more likely lose his life looking for us, than gain happiness finding us.

The Brotherhood of the Rosy Cross

Chemical Wedding: Christian Rosencreutz

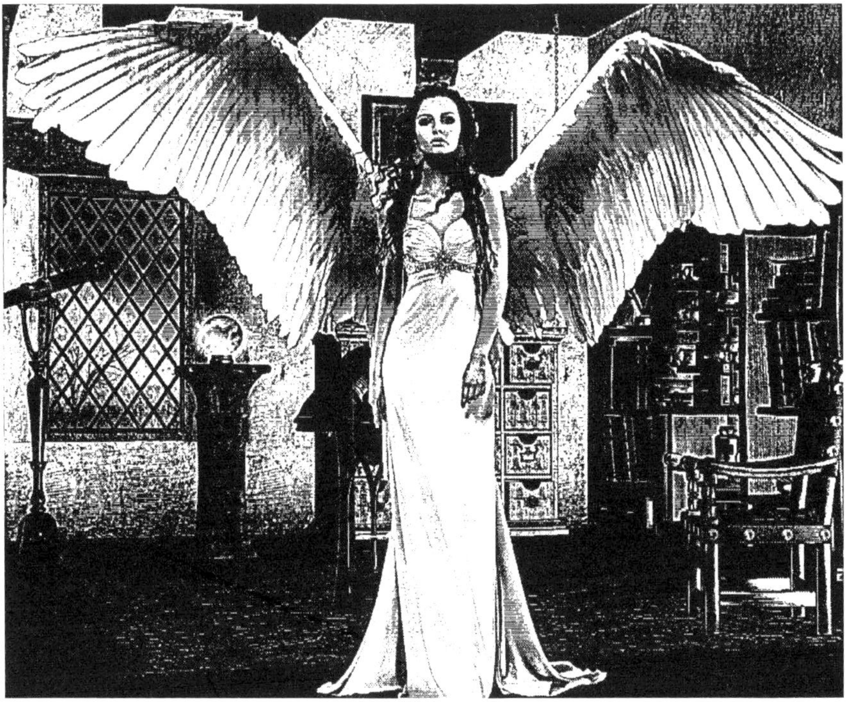

Chapter One

The First Day

One evening before Easter Day, I sat down to eat. I had spoken at length with my creator through my usual humble prayers and had also meditated upon many great mysteries (the father of lights, in his majesty, had shown me quite a few of those!). I was also ready to prepare, in my heart, a small and perfect piece of unleavened cake to accompany my lovely Paschal lamb.

Suddenly, a terrible storm arose. It was so fierce that I imagined the entire hill on which my little house was built would be torn to pieces!

But despite this, I took heart and continued with my meditation. I was used to this and similar antics from the Devil (who was always troubling me).

Then I felt someone touch me on my back.

I was terrified and hardly dared to turn around. Bracing myself, I tried to look as cheerful as I could manage under the circumstances. It tugged my coat again several times and I looked around.

There was a beautiful and glorious lady, dressed in sky-coloured clothes which were strangely glittering with golden stars like the heavens.

In her right hand she held a trumpet of beaten gold and there was a name engraved on it. I could clearly see this name but I am forbidden to reveal what it was at the moment. In her left hand she had a great bundle of letters written in all languages which she (as I was told later) would carry to all countries.

She also had large and beautiful wings, which were covered with eyes. With these, she could take to the skies and fly swifter than an eagle.

I probably would have noticed more about her but she was only with me for a short time and I was overcome with fear and surprise.

For, as soon as I had turned around, she leafed through her letters before finally taking out a small one, which with great reverence she laid down upon the table. She then left without a word but, in taking to the air, gave a mighty blast on her noble trumpet, which made the whole hill echo with the sound. So much so, that I could barely hear myself speak for over a quarter of an hour.

I was totally at a loss for what to do next in this unexpected adventure. So I fell upon my knees and begged my creator to stop anything happening to me that would prevent my getting into heaven.

Then, with fear and trepidation, I went over to pick up the letter. It was so heavy it could not have weighed more even if it had been made from pure gold.

As I carefully examined the letter, I noticed a small seal in the shape of a peculiar kind of cross with this inscription:

'IN HOC SIGNO ☫ VINCES' (*In this sign ☫ he shall conquer*).

As soon as I saw this, I was quite relieved knowing that a seal such as this would be despised and never used by the Devil.

And so I opened the letter with great care and there inside, written in golden letters on an azure blue background were the following verses[59]:

'Today. Today. Today

is the King's Wedding Day.

If you were born for this and chosen by God; You may go the mountain where three temples stand and witness it from there.

Be vigilant, take care as, if you do not bathe thoroughly, the Wedding may bring about your ruin.

Ruin comes to he who fails in this – take care that your weight is enough'.

Below was written:

Groom and Bride (Sponsus et Sponsa)

When I had finished reading, I almost fainted. My hair stood on end and a cold sweat trickled down my entire body.

For I realised that this was the prearranged wedding which was shown to me seven years before in a physical vision. I had waited for a long time and made careful calculations by observing and studying the planets. Yet I had never guessed that it would finally happen in such terrifying and dangerous times.

Before this, I had always imagined that in order to be a welcome and acceptable guest, I only needed to turn up the wedding. Now, I had been shown that it involved divine fate. Until this moment, I was not sure of this.

I also discovered that, the more I questioned myself, my head was filled with nothing but ignorance and misunderstanding and I was blind to mysterious things. So much so, that I could not even understand what was right before my eyes every day! I had no idea why I, of all people, should be dedicated to seeking out and understanding the secrets of nature.

In my opinion, I thought that nature would consider that almost anyone else in the world would make a better and more virtuous disciple than me! I would have expected her to entrust her precious but transient treasures to someone else.

I also found that my outward behaviour, speech and brotherly love towards my neighbour was not always pure and free from motive. As well as this, my worldly desires were often manifested in displays of pride and showing off, which is <u>not</u> for the good of mankind. I was always on the lookout to make a quick profit or increase my status, build stately palaces, make myself famous and other similar carnal desires.

But the mysterious words concerning the three temples troubled me the most. I could not make head nor tail of it (and possibly would still have not have been able to, if they had not been so wonderfully revealed to me).

Stuck somewhere between hope and fear, I tried to analyse myself again but found only weakness and failings. I was unable to help myself and was overcome by this fear, so I tried the safest and most reliable course of action. After I had finished my sincere and passionate prayers, I lay in bed with the hope that (as had occasionally happened before), my good angel would appear to me, God willing, and give me advice on these unresolved matters. And, to the praise of God, my own welfare and as a warning to my neighbours of the changes to come, this is what happened:

I had scarcely fallen asleep when I felt myself chained up in a dark dungeon along with countless other men. Without even a glimmer of light, we swarmed like bees over one another, which only made the suffering worse.

Although none of us could see a thing, there was the constant sound of one man hauling himself over another whenever his chains and manacles would even slightly allow it but none of us had much of a reason to clamber over another since we were all miserably imprisoned.

This suffering continued for quite some time with each man complaining about his own blindness and captivity until we heard the sound of many trumpets sounding and the steady beat of kettle drums. This broke the spell of our suffering and we rejoiced at the sound. As this great noise sounded, the cover of the dungeon was lifted and a crack of light became visible.

For the first time our frenzied activity could be clearly seen - all hell broke loose, as he who had pulled himself up too much was forced down again and under the others' feet. In short – each man struggled to get to the top. I did not hold back either, I freed my heavy chains from under the others then caught hold of a stone and dragged myself upwards. Others were grabbing at me and I was caught hold of several times but defended myself with hands and feet.

We all thought that we had been set free but it was turning out to be quite the opposite.

The noblemen who looked down upon us through the hole observed our struggles and shouts and, after a while, a grey-haired old man yelled at us to be quiet. No sooner had silence fallen than (as I still recall to this day) he began to speak to us:

'If the human race was not so arrogant, my mother's heritage would have given it many good things. But, because the human race will not listen, it ends up held captive in this dire situation.

Despite this, my dearest mother ignores this misbehaviour. She leaves her beautiful gifts so that many men may come to the light. But it is only occasionally that these gifts are valued or seen as anything but fictional.

Therefore, in honour of the feast, which we are holding today and to increase her goodwill, she will do this good deed: The rope will now be lowered. Whoever can hang on to it will be freed'.

He had barely finished speaking when an old woman ordered her servants to let down the rope seven times into the dungeon and bring up anyone who could hang on.

Good God! I cannot even begin to describe the commotion and distress that broke out upon us hearing this. Everyone struggled to get to the rope but only held each other back. After seven minutes, a little bell rang and the servants brought up four on the first pull. At that time, I could not get anywhere near to the rope because (as I mentioned earlier) I had climbed onto a stone in the dungeon wall and could not get to the rope, which came down in the middle.

They lowered the rope for a second time. But many, because their chains were too heavy and their hands sore, could not keep their grip on the rope. They ended up knocking down others who might have been able to hold on otherwise. Even in our mutual misery we were still jealous of others and many were forcibly pulled down by others who were themselves unable to get near.

But the ones I felt sorriest for and moved by were those whose weight was so heavy that they tore their own hands from their bodies, attempting to get up.

And so, after five turns, very few had been drawn up because as soon as the sign was given, the servants were very quick in drawing up the rope. Most of the men tumbled down on each other and the rope was drawn up almost empty.

After this, the majority of us, including myself, despaired of being saved. We called upon God to have pity and if possible, save us from this limbo.

He must have heard some of us. For, when the rope came down for the sixth time, some of them held fast. Whilst the rope was being drawn up, it swung from one side to the other and, perhaps by the will of God, it came to me and I caught hold of it. I was higher than all the rest and finally, beyond my wildest hopes, came out at the top. I was so ecstatic with joy that I did not even notice a wound on my head, which I had received from a sharp stone whilst being drawn up. As had happened on each occasion, those freed had to help with the seventh and last pull. When I had finished this, the strain had caused the wound to bleed and there was blood all over my clothes, which I was too happy to even notice.

When this last pull, which had brought up most of all, had finished, the old woman made them put the rope to one side and asked her aged son to tell the rest of the prisoners what her purpose was. After he had thought for a little while he spoke:

'Dear children. You who are here. What has been recognized for a long time is now completed. The great favour that my mother has shown you here should not be disrespected. A joyful time is coming soon. When all people will be equal and no one will be poor or rich. And those who were given important tasks now have much to contribute. And those who were trusted and given a lot will be stripped bare. So forget your sorrows, it is only a few days away.'

As soon as he had spoken these words, the cover was replaced and locked down and the trumpets and kettle drums began again. But even their noise was not enough to drown out the pitiful cries of the prisoners left in the dungeon and I was soon in tears.

Soon after, the old woman, together with her son, sat on seats that had been placed there and ordered that those saved should be counted. She asked for everyone's name and it was written down on a little golden-yellow tablet by a servant.

She looked at us all, one after the other and sighed before speaking to her son, loudly enough so I too could hear what she said.

'I am so terribly sorry for the poor men in the dungeon! I wish to God I could release them all.'

'It is God's rule, Mother', her son replied 'And we cannot argue. If every single one of us were lords and owned all of the things on earth and then all sat down to dine, who would be left to serve us?'.

His mother was quiet for a while but soon after, she spoke 'Well, at least let these men be freed from their chains'.

This was done and I was nearly the last to be freed. Although there were still others to be released, I could not help myself and bowed before the old woman, giving thanks to God that, through her, he had so kindly granted it that I had been brought out of darkness and into the light. After I had done this, the others did the same, which pleased the old lady.

Finally, everyone was given a commemorative piece of gold, which could be spent. On one side was stamped the rising sun and on the other (as I recall) these three letters: D.L.S.[60]

And then, everyone was allowed to leave and sent about his business on this condition: That we should work for the glory of God to benefit our neighbours and to keep it secret, as we had promised to do. And so we went our separate ways.

But because of the wounds caused by my shackles, I had difficulty walking and stopped still. The old woman saw me, let out a laugh and then called me over to her.

She said to me 'My Son, don't let this affect you. Embrace your weaknesses and thank God who has allowed you to exist that, even in your imperfect state you have come to so high a light. Keep these wounds for me'.

Suddenly the trumpets began to sound again which gave me such a shock that I woke up and realised it was only a dream. But it had been so vivid that I was still anxious about it and I thought that I could still feel the wounds on my feet.

However, because of all of this, I understood clearly that God had granted it that I should attend this proposed mysterious wedding.

Due to this, with a naive confidence I thanked his divine majesty and asked that he would continue to keep me fearing him and that every day he would fill my heart with wisdom and understanding and finally, stay with me and lead me to the ultimate goal, undeserving as I was.

After this I got ready for the journey by putting on my white linen coat, binding a blood-red ribbon across my shoulder and mentally preparing myself. I stuck four red roses in my hat so I could be easily distinguished in a crowd by this sign. For food I took bread, salt and water, as a seasoned traveller had once advised me and as I had successfully done before in similar circumstances.

But before I left my cottage I fell to my knees in these clothes and wedding garment and prayed to God that, whatever might happen he would grant me a happy ending.

And there, in the presence of God, I vowed that if anything were revealed to me by his grace, that I would use it not for my own advancement or honour but for his glory and the service of my neighbour.

With this vow and with high hopes, I happily left my house.

CHAPTER ONE – NOTES

[59] The seal on the letter is best known by the name 'Monas Heiroglyphica' and is associated with John Dee, the occultist famed as an advisor to Queen Elizabeth I. Dee wrote a book explaining the significance of the symbol in 1564. I will not attempt to tackle the deeper layers of its symbolism here but it can be broken down into four main components.

Each of these symbols has its own distinct meaning:

- MOON
- SUN
- 4 ELEMENTS
- FIRE

[60] Notes on the margin of the 1616 Strasbourg printing records D.L.S. in this manner:

Deus Lux Solis – *God, the divine sunlight.* Deo Laus Semper – *Always Praise God.* (Nummus aureus is '*a gold coin*'). It is unclear who wrote the notes and the explanation of D.L.S. does not appear in the main text so these are only possible definitions and not definitive.

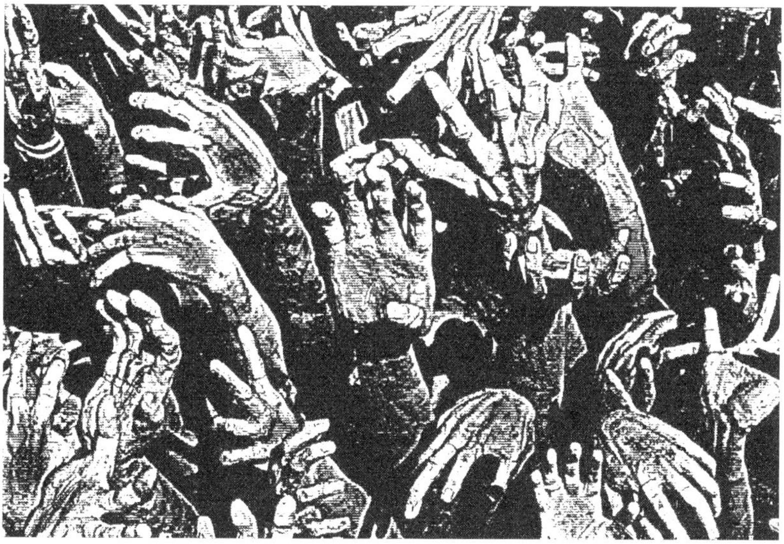

CHAPTER TWO

Chapter Two

The Second Day

I had hardly left my house and entered a forest when I felt that the whole of heaven and all of the elements had already prepared themselves beautifully for this wedding. For even the birds sang more sweetly than ever before and the young fawns skipped so merrily that they filled my heart with joy and I broke loudly into song:

Be happy dear bird
And praise your maker,
Sing bright and clear
Your God is most high.

He has prepared your food for you
To give to you at the right season

So be content with this,
Why would you not be glad?
Will you blame God
For making you a bird?

Will it worry your little head
That he didn't make you a man?
Be calm, he has thought it all through,
And be content.

What do I have to do, a worm of the earth
To argue with God?

As though I in this heaven's storm
Had the power to resist.
You cannot fight God.
Whoever, thinks he can, let him be taken away.

Oh man, be satisfied,
That he did not make you the king

And do not take it the wrong way;
If you hated him for it,
It would be a very bad thing:
Because God has clearer eyes than that –
He looks into your heart
And you cannot deceive Him

From the bottom of my heart, I sang this throughout the whole forest, so loudly that it echoed from the hills. Eventually, I came to the edge of the forest and leaving it, entered a strange, green heath.

Three tall cedars stood on this lovely heath and they were of such a size to provide me with plenty of welcome shade. Although I had not yet travelled very far, my intense desire was quite overwhelming and I hurried to the trees so I could rest for a little while.

But as I got nearer, I saw a tablet attached to one of the trees. On it was a strange inscription:

'Hello Guest! If you have heard anything about the king's wedding, take note of these words.

Through us, the Bridegroom offers you four paths; If you do not fail, all of them can lead you to his royal court.

The first path is short but dangerous. It will lead you into rocky places. These are nearly impossible to pass.

The second is longer and takes you around the obstacles – it is plain and easy if you use the magnet to stick to the path and not turn off.

The third is the truly royal way, which, through the king's various pleasures and parades, makes for a very pleasant journey. However, this is hard to get into and barely one in a thousand are accepted.

No man can reach the place using the fourth path because it is designed only for indestructible beings.

Now – choose which of the three paths you wish to follow and stick with it. Know that, whichever you enter, that is the one that fate has chosen for you. You cannot turn back without great risk to your life.

These are the things we wish to tell you.

But beware! You cannot even begin to understand the dangers you may face with this commitment. If you know that you are unworthy or at fault according to the laws of our king, even in the slightest way, we beg you to turn back now and return to your home, whilst you still can...'

As soon as I read this, my heart sank. I, who had been happily singing a short time ago, began to despair. Because, even though I saw all three ways before me and understood that it was taken for granted that I would choose one, I was worried:

If I chose the rocky road, I could well be killed in a fall.

If I took the long way, I might wander off the path or get delayed on the route.

I could not hope to be lucky enough to be accepted out of thousands of others if I chose the royal path.

I also saw the fourth path in front of me but it was alive with fire and other dangers, so much so, that I didn't even dare to go near to it.

Again and again, I considered whether to take the paths before me or to give up and turn back.

I thought about my unworthiness but I was comforted by the dream – I *had* been saved from the tower, after all. And yet, it was just a dream and I couldn't rely on it.

I was so confused by all of this that I suddenly felt very tired, hungry and thirsty, so I cut myself a slice of bread. A snow-white dove sitting in the tree had seen this. Without my noticing she flew down. She hopped over to me in a tame and friendly way and I was happy to share my food with her. I felt lifted by the sight of this pretty, little bird. But then, a jet-black raven who had spotted the food flew down and pushed aside the dove, taking her food. The dove could not defend herself or the food, other than by taking flight and both birds flew off towards the south. I was suddenly furious and chased after the filthy raven. Without realising it, I ran an entire length of a field along one of the four pathways before I had scared off the raven and saved the dove.

I then looked around and realised what I had done; I had entered into one of the ways and could not go back without the risk of severe punishment.

Before I could calm myself, I realized what was worst of all was that I had left my bag and bread at the tree and now could never get them back because, as soon as I turned back, a wind blew against me so strongly that I was nearly blown away. However, if I continued forwards, there was no hindrance at all.

It was obvious that I would be killed if I tried to fight against the wind so, I decided to bear this cross. I got to my feet, determined that, if this is how it must be, that I would make my best efforts to get to the end of my journey before dark.

There were many side-roads on the route but I continued straight on according to my compass and did not budge one step from the meridian line; although, sometimes the road was rough and seemed almost impassable to me.

Along the way, I constantly thought about the dove and the raven but I could not work out the meaning.

After a while, I saw a majestic gate on a high hill, far in the distance. The sun was already below the hills and, seeing no other place to go, I hurried towards it, not caring how far away it was or in what direction it took me. I put this down only to God, who may well have allowed me to proceed in this way and directed my eyes away from anything but this gate.

I hurried on towards it and finally reached it whilst there was still enough daylight remaining to get a good look at it. It was a majestic and incredibly beautiful doorway on which was carved a multitude of noble figures and emblems, every one of which (as I later learned) having a unique meaning.

Above the doorway was a quite large tablet showing the words 'keep away, you who are profane' ('*Procul hinc, procul ite profani*'), as well as other things that I have been forbidden to tell you.

As soon as I stood before the door, a person wearing a sky-blue robe immediately stepped forward. I greeted him and, thankfully, he returned my friendly greeting but then demanded my letter of invitation.

Oh, how glad I was that I still had it with me! It would have been so easy to have forgotten it (as, it turned out, others had before me, according to the man!)

I quickly presented it and he was not only satisfied with it but also (to my great surprise) showed me a lot of respect, asking my name and saying 'Come in my brother, you are my very welcome guest'.

Having said to him that I was a Brother of the Red-Rosy Cross he seemed both happy and surprised.

He said 'My Brother, do you have anything on you that you can use to buy a token?'

I answered that I had very little but if there was anything of mine that he could use, he was welcome to it. He asked for my bottle of water, which I happily gave to him.

In return, he handed me a golden token with nothing inscribed on it but the two letters S.C.[61] He urged me to remember him if ever I needed recommendation.

After this, I asked him how many had come in before I did, which he answered. As a token of friendship, he handed me a sealed letter for the second porter.

I had spent some time with him and the night grew darker. A great beacon was lit up on the gate so that if anyone else was still on the path, they could quickly make their way towards it.

The length of road finished at the castle. It was enclosed by walls on either side and lined with all kinds of fruit trees. There were lanterns hung on every third tree and the candles were then touched and lit by a beautiful maiden dressed in sky-blue. It was such a majestic and glorious sight that I stayed to watch for much longer than I had intended.

Eventually, after directions, information and helpful advice, I gave a fond farewell to the first porter and left.

On my way, I would have loved to have known what was written in my letter but, as I had no reason to mistrust the porter, put these thoughts aside and continued until I came to the second gate. This gate was very much like the other and decorated with images and mystical symbols. On the tablet was written '*Date et dabitur vobis*' ('give and it shall be given to you').

Chained under the gate was a fierce lion. As soon as the lion saw me, he came after me, roaring loudly. This woke the second porter who had been lying on a marble slab. He told me not to be afraid and not to worry and called off the lion. I handed over the letter with trembling hands and he opened and read it. He then said to me 'Welcome, in God's name, to a man for whom I have been waiting a long time'[62].

He drew out a token and asked if I could pay for it. I had nothing left but my salt so I gave this to him and he happily accepted it, handing me the token. This token had the letters S.M.[63] upon it.

I was just about to talk to him when a loud ringing sounded. The Porter turned to me and told me to run or else all my efforts would be wasted. As I rushed off, he warned me that the lights were going out. But I did not hear what else he said as I was in such a panic. Behind the maiden, the lights were being extinguished and I would never have found my way if it wasn't for the light of her torch. I could only go so fast however, and ended up going through the gate at the same time as the maiden. The gate suddenly slammed shut catching my coat in it. I could not pull it free. Some of the others outside and I all called to the porter but despite this, he would not open it again. He said he had handed the keys to the maiden who had taken them into the court. I was forced to leave my coat behind.

I looked at the gate once more, which now appeared so rich that nothing in the whole world could equal it. Just by the door stood two columns. On one stood a pleasant figure with the inscription 'Congratulor' (Congratulations). The other was shrouded and sad and written beneath was the word 'Condoleo' (Condolences)[64].

In short, the inscriptions and figures were so dark and mysterious that the most talented man on earth could not have explained them. But I will explain all of them very soon, if God permits.

Under this gate, I was asked for my name again. This time though, it was written down in a little vellum book and sent, with the others, to the Lord Bridegroom.

It was here that I received the real guest token. It was smaller than the other tokens but much heavier. On it was the letters S.P.N.[65]

I was also given a new pair of shoes as the floor of the castle was made with pure shining marble.
I gave away my old shoes to an old man in the crowd of poor people who sat quietly under the gate. Two pages bearing torches then led me to a small room.

They asked me to sit, which I did. Then they placed their torches in two holes in the pavement and left me sitting alone.

After a while, I heard a noise but did not see anything. It turned out to be some men who had come into the room but they were invisible. They were jostling me around but I could not see anyone so waited to see what they were up to. It turned out that they were barbers and I begged them not to shove me about so much as I'd do whatever they wanted me to do. They suddenly let go of me. One of them (I still could not see them) gently trimmed the hair at the crown of my head. He left my grey hair alone over my forehead and around my ears and eyes.

During this whole encounter, I almost despaired as I could not see anything and they were shoving me around quite forcefully. I thought that I had failed God due to my curiosity.

The invisible barbers gathered up the cut hair and carried it away.

The two pages returned and were laughing at me because I had been so scared. We hardly had chance to talk before a little bell began to ring. The pages said it was calling an assembly and asked me to stand and go with them. We made our way along many corridors, through doors and on winding stairs until we entered a spacious hall.

In this room was a great gathering of guests; emperors, kings, princes, lords, noble and common, rich and poor – all sorts of people.

I was filled with wonder and thought to myself 'Ah, how stupid you have been; to make this journey with so much trouble and strain! Look, here are people you know well, whom you have never had any particular reason to admire but they are all here. And you, with all your prayers and devotion barely made it!'.

The Devil put these thoughts and more into my head whilst I tried my best to concentrate on the matter in hand.

Meanwhile, some of my acquaintances who I knew a little came over and one of them spoke to me.

'Oh, Brother Rosencreutz! You're here too?'

'Yes, my Brothers' I replied 'The grace of God has helped me get in'.

They responded by roaring with laughter. They thought it was ridiculous that God should be needed for such a minor thing.

So, I asked them to tell me about their journeys and found out that most of them were forced to climb over the rocks. Then, the sound of trumpets indicated that we should sit. They all considered themselves more important and every one of them sat themselves in places on the top table. For me and a few other sorry guests, there was barely any space left even on the lowest table.

Shortly, the two Pages entered and one of them said grace. He spoke it in such a beautiful way that it lifted my heart.

However, certain 'senior fellows' were incredibly rude, ignoring them and sniggering, joking and winking throughout.

After the grace, invisible hands brought in food. Although we could not see anyone, it was so organised and smooth, it seemed to me as if every single guest had his own server.

After they had eaten a little, my fellows, having had their inhibitions lifted by the wine, began to show off, boasting of their abilities. One of them would 'prove' this and another that. However, it is usually the empty vessel that makes the loudest noise…

When I remember all the superhuman feats and impossible adventures I heard of, I still come close to throwing up. Every opportunity they had to ingratiate themselves with the nobility, one and then another would be chiming in. They pretended to have completed amazing adventures that not even Hercules or Samson could have managed. One would relieve Atlas of his burden, and then another would have dragged the three-headed Cerberus out of Hell. In a nutshell, each one had his own foolish boast but the greatest lords were so gullible that they believed every outrageous claim. It was as if even though every now and again, one of them was rapped on the knuckles, they just ignored it and carried on. And then, every time one of them scored points the others would try to do the same, regardless of consequences.

One said he heard the rustling of the heavens. A second could see Plato's ideas. A third could count Democritus's atoms. More than one claimed to have achieved perpetual motion! Many of them, in my opinion, had a good understanding but spoiled it by taking too much credit for themselves.

Finally, one had the audacity to try to persuade us that he could see the invisible servants who attended us. He might have done it too but one of the invisible waiters gave him such a slap that he and many more around him, immediately shut up!

What pleased me though was that those for whom I had respect were very quiet and humble. They admitted that they did not know everything and that the mysteries of nature were beyond their own abilities.

In all the commotion, I nearly cursed the day I came here; because I could not help but notice that all the loud and conceited people were at the top tables. To make it worse, even at the lowest place I could not have any peace because one of the cheeky show-offs sneeringly called me an idiot.

Now, little did I realise that we still had one more gate to pass. I thought that I would have to put up with this scorn, contempt and indignity throughout the whole wedding even though I had not done anything to the Lord Bridegroom or Bride to deserve this.

Because of this, it was my opinion that he should have picked some other fool to come to his wedding.

You can see how impatient the unfairness of the world can make simple hearts such as mine. But this is only one of my weaknesses.

The longer the racket continued, the louder it got. There were already enough people there boasting of imaginary visions without others now trying to convince us of their clearly made-up dreams.

Sat by me was a very nice and quiet man who talked about some really interesting topics. Eventually he said 'Look. My Brother – if anyone came in now and offered to teach these ignorant people the right way, do you think they would take any notice?'

'Not at all' I replied

'The world' he said 'has now convinced itself to be cheated and will not listen to those with good intentions. Do you see that show-off taking in people by using fancy words and appealing to foolish vanity? Or that one making fun of people using mysterious words he has just made up? Trust me; it will not be long before these awful frauds are shown to the world for what they are. Then perhaps, there will be some value placed on the things that are disrespected now'.

Whilst he was talking, the noise in the hall grew worse. Suddenly, the most excellent and stately music I had ever heard in my life began to play. The room fell silent.

The music combined every stringed instrument imaginable, sounding together in such beautiful harmony that I forgot myself, lost in the music. I sat so still that those around me were amazed at the sight and it lasted for almost half an hour, with not one person speaking a single word. If anyone attempted to open their mouths, they promptly received an unexpected blow from some invisible assailant. We were clearly not permitted to see the musicians but I remember thinking that I would have loved to have seen all the instruments they were playing, at least.

After half an hour, the music stopped suddenly and we could not see or hear anything else.

Shortly afterwards, a great noise began at the door of the hall, with trumpets, kettledrums and other instruments, as majestic as if the emperor of Rome were arriving. The door opened by itself and the noise of the trumpets became almost too much to bear.

Meanwhile, thousands (by my count) of small tapers came into the hall, marching by themselves in strict formation. Finally, the two pages from before entered bearing very bright torches and lighting the way for an incredibly beautiful maiden, drawn on a wonderful, glorious, golden throne which moved by itself.

It appeared to me that this was the very same maiden I had seen before, who lit and extinguished the lanterns and her attendants were those whom she had placed at the trees. She was no longer in sky-blue but now wore a glittering snow-white robe which sparkled with pure gold and shone so brightly we could scarcely look at it.

Both pages were dressed in a similar manner (but much more modestly).

As soon as they came into the middle of the hall, she descended from the throne and all of the small tapers bowed before her.

We all stood up in our places respectfully. She, having shown us the same respect and reverence as we had shown to her, she began to speak to us in a pleasant tone:

The King, my gracious lord
Is not far away,
Nor is his dearest bride,

Betrothed to him in honour.

They have now with the greatest joy
Seen you arriving here.
They would especially like to offer
Their approval to each of you,
And wish with all their hearts
That you will always prosper
And that of the coming wedding brings you only joy
With nothing to spoil it.

At this, she paused, courteously bowed in unison with the tapers and soon continued:

You know what it says in the invitation;
No man has been called here
Unless he has already received
All the most beautiful gifts from God
And has properly dressed himself
Befitting this occasion.

Although some might not believe it
That anyone would be so reckless
Given these conditions
To turn up
When he has not prepared himself

For this wedding, well in advance.

So, now they stand hoping
That you will be provided with all good things.
Be glad that, in these hard times
So many such people can be found.

But men are so presumptuous
That they do not care about their rudeness
And thrust themselves into places
They have no reason to be.
Let no unscrupulous man be let in,
No dishonest man sneak in with others.

They will openly say
That they will have a pure wedding.
So, tomorrow morning
The artist will set his scales
And weigh each one
To find what he has forgotten.

Of all the crowd assembled here,
If you do not trust him to do this
You must stand aside now.

And if you stay here any longer

You will lose all goodwill and credit,

And be trampled underfoot.

And anyone with a guilty conscience

Will be left in this hall today

And freed tomorrow

But will never be allowed to return.

But he who knows his value

Let him go with his servant

Who will take him to his room

And there he may rest for today

As he awaits the scales' approval.

Otherwise, he will not sleep well.

Let the others be comfortable here

For he who has stretched his resources

Would be better to have hidden away.

We hope for the best from each one of you.

As soon as she had said this, she bowed again and cheerfully sprang back into her throne. The trumpets sounded again but more quietly than before and she was invisibly escorted away. Most of the tapers remained in the room and accompanied each one of us.

Amongst the resulting anxiety it was impossible to say what each of us was thinking. However, most of us were determined to wait for the scales and hoped that we would be allowed to leave in peace if this did not go well.

I had weighed up my options and, because my conscience had convinced me that I was ignorant and unworthy, I decided to stay with the others in the hall, choosing to be content with the meal I had received rather than run the risk of rejection.

After everyone had been conducted into a chamber by his taper (one per person as I understood), only nine of us were left which included the man I had been talking with at the table. Although our tapers did not leave us, after an hour or so, one of the Pages came back with a great bundle of cords. He asked us to confirm if we had decided to stay in the hall, which we did with sighs. He used the cords to tie each one of us to a particular place and left together with the tapers, leaving us in darkness.

Then, some of us began to feel the strain. For myself, I broke down in tears. Although we had not been forbidden to speak, we felt so sorrowful that not one of use could bring himself to utter a word. The cords that bound us had been made with such skill that they could not be neither cut nor removed from our feet. It comforted me a little to think that, of many of those who had been taken to rest, they would not get the results that they expected when it came down to it.

We, on the other hand, by a single night of penance, might at least make amends for our arrogance.

Finally, despite my sad thoughts, I fell asleep and dreamed. Although this is not a big deal, I think it is relevant if I give an account of it.

I thought I was upon a high mountain, and saw before me a great and wide valley. In this valley were gathered a vast crowd of people, each one suspended from heaven by a thread attached to their heads. Some were hanging high up, some low, some almost standing on the earth.

Through the air, an ancient man flew up and down. He had a pair of shears, which he used to cut some of the people's cords. Those that were close to the earth fell silently but when it happened to somebody high up, he or she fell so hard that the earth shook.

The threads of some stretched out so much that, even before the thread was cut, they touched the earth.

I greatly enjoyed watching them tumble down and was ecstatic when one of those who had thought themselves so important to the wedding had such a disgraceful fall that he took some of his neighbours with him.

It also made me greatly happy to see that those who had kept themselves close to the ground came down so lightly and gently that even the men right next to them did not notice.

At my very happiest moment, I was accidentally knocked and woken up by one of my fellow captives. I felt very annoyed with him. However, I thought about my dream and told my Brother who was lying on the other side of me. He was interested to hear it and hoped that it may have been meant to give me some comfort. We chatted about this for the rest of the night, longing for the new day.

CHAPTER TWO: NOTES

[61] As with D.L.S. in the previous chapter, the 1616 Strasbourg printing has the following annotations for S.C.:

1. Sanctitate consta(n)tia - (Constancy in holiness)
2. Sponsus charus (Sponsus carus) – The dear bridegroom
3. Spes, Charitas (Spes, Caritas) – Hope, Charity

It is hard to know what to make of these annotations. If they are by the author (possibly Johann Andreae) then you would expect him to have placed it in the main text and to have made the intended meaning clear rather than giving three differing options. As it is, these annotations can only be regarded as speculative and by an unknown hand.

[62] This Porter says that our hero is the man he has long waited to see. This suggests it is the Porter from the end of the tale who is released from his servitude due to the forthcoming actions taken by Christian. It therefore suggests that the events of the future are predetermined.

[63] Annotations suggest:

1. Studio merentis, Sal humor. 'The study was worthy, Salt humours'. John Purcell M.D. Refers to 'Salt Humours' in his work 'A Treatise of the Cholick' published in 1714.
2. Sponso mittendus 'To be given to the bridegroom'
3. Sal mineralis 'Mineral salt'
4. Sal menstrualis 'Menstrual salt'

[64] The pillars directly translate as 'I congratulate' and 'I condole' respectively.

[65] Annotations suggest:

1. Salus per naturam 'Salvation through nature'
2. Sponsi praesentandus nuptiis 'To be given at the bridegroom's wedding'

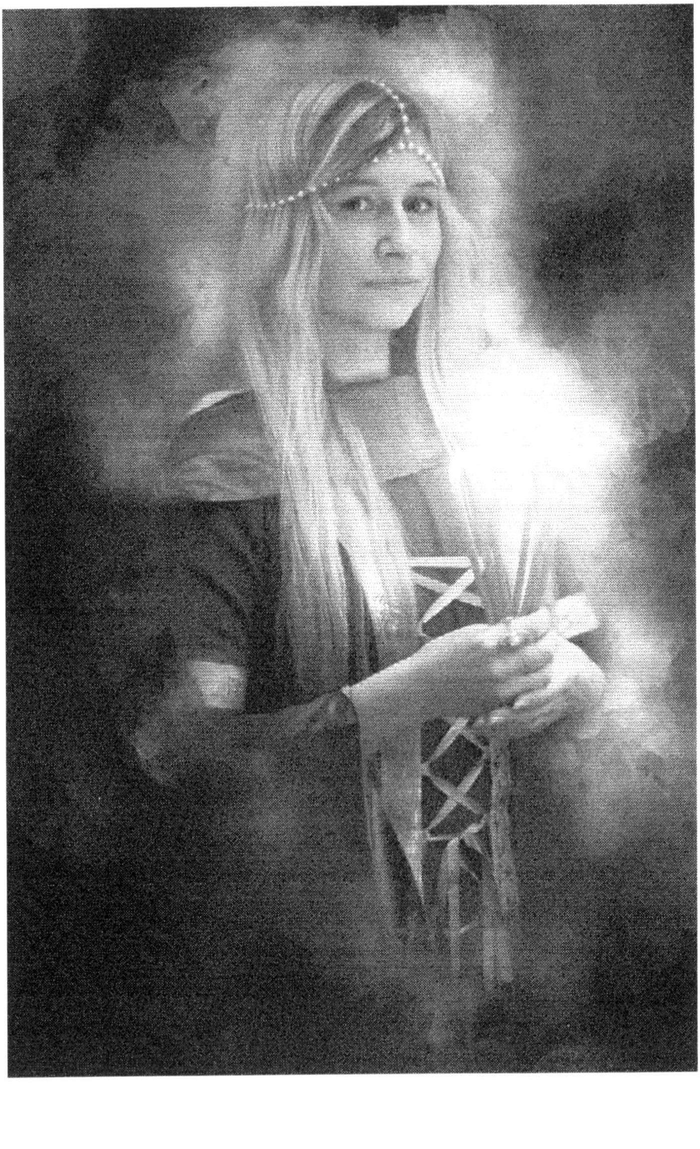

Chapter Three

The Third Day

The daybreak was beautiful and the bright sun rose above the hills to his appointed spot in the high heaven. My good companions began to get up and in a leisurely manner made themselves ready for the inquisition.

One after another, they came into the hall, saying 'Good morning' and asking us how we had slept. Some of them, having seen our bonds, told us off for being so cowardly as, unlike them, we had not dared to take this adventure.

However, some whose hearts troubled them were more subdued.

We openly admitted our ignorance and said that we hoped that we would soon be freed and that we would be wiser for our disgrace. We added that they, on the other hand, were not finished yet and their greatest danger may be yet to come.

Eventually, everyone was assembled again and the trumpets began to sound and the kettle drums beat as before.

We imagined that the Bridegroom would now enter but this was a huge mistake. The Maiden from yesterday once more appeared before us but this time was wearing red velvet with a white scarf around her waist. On her head was a green wreath of laurel leaves, which really suited her looks.

She was not accompanied by small tapers this time but by two hundred men in armour who, like her, were clothed in red and white.

She came down from her throne and walked directly to us prisoners, saluting us before speaking.

'Some of you are aware of your own sad state and this is greatly pleasing to my most mighty lord. He is determined that you will do well because of it.'

She then noticed my clothes and laughing, she said to me 'Goodness! Have you joined the ranks of the humble too? I thought you were more the smug type'.

Her words caused my eyes to well up with tears.

She commanded that we be untied and taken to a position where we would have a good view of the scales. She said that it might even work out better for us than with some of those who still stood here free.

In the meantime, the scales, which were entirely gilded in gold, were hung up in the middle of the hall. There was also a little table covered with red velvet and seven weights were placed upon it. There was one, quite large weight, four little ones and two huge ones. These weights were unbelievably heavier than their sizes suggested.

She organised each of the armoured men into seven groups, one for each of the weights. Each armoured man, as well as his unsheathed sword, had a strong rope. She then mounted her throne.

As soon as she had bowed, she began to speak in a piercing tone:

Whoever goes into an artist's room
And knows nothing of painting
But speaks as if he is expert
Will soon be mocked by everyone.

And he who joins an artists' group
Without being selected
And makes a big show of his painting
Will soon be mocked by everyone.

And he who comes to a wedding
Without being asked
Yet comes making a big show of it
Will soon be mocked by everyone.

And he who climbs upon these scales
And finds he does not make the weight
But gets shot upwards with a mighty crash
Will soon be mocked by everyone.

As soon as the Maiden had finished talking, one of the pages commanded that each person should place themselves according to their rank and step forwards one by one.

Without hesitation, one of the emperors stepped forwards, bowed slightly to the Maiden and went up in all his grand clothes. Then, each captain put a weight on the scales. To everyone's surprise, he held out until the last weight, which was too heavy for him and he was told to leave. He was so distressed as he stepped down that (as it seemed to me) the Maiden herself took pity on him and indicated her people to be quiet. All the same, the good emperor was bound and taken to the sixth band.

Next, there came another emperor, who proudly stepped onto the scale. He had hidden a big, thick book under his gown and thought that he would not fail but he could not even take the third weight and was unmercifully flung off. The book fell out of his robes, causing the soldiers to laugh at him! He was bound and taken to the third band.

And so it continued with some of the other emperors who were unmercifully laughed at and tied up.

After these, a short man with a curly brown beard stepped forward. He was also an emperor and, after paying the usual respects, got onto the scale. He held out so firmly that I thought, even if more weights had been available, he still would have outweighed them.

The Maiden immediately rose and bowed before him. She made him wear a gown of red velvet and gave him a laurel branch from a large stock she had by the throne. She invited him to sit down on the steps below her throne.

As for the rest of the emperors, kings and lords – this would take too long to describe but I must say that few of these 'great men' held out. However, many of them showed some noble virtues (beyond my expectations).

One could hold out against this, the second another. Some two, some three, four or five but very few could achieve perfection and every one that failed was mocked by the bands.

The inquisition had examined the gentry, the learned and unlearned and all the rest and in each case one, maybe two but mostly none had been found perfect. It was now time for those 'honest gentlemen' the travelling cheaters and lowlife '*Lapidem Spitalanficum*' (quack medicine) makers. They were put on the scales with such contempt that I, in spite of all my sorrows, was laughing fit to burst, as were the other prisoners. Most of them could not stand the severe trial and were beaten from the scales with whips and scourges then led to the other prisoners and to their appropriate band.

And of so great a crowd, so few remained that I am embarrassed to reveal the total.

However, there were many people of quality amongst them who, like the others, were honoured with velvet robes and laurel leaves.

The Inquisition having finished and none except us poor tied-up hounds standing, one of the captains stepped forward and said

'Gracious madam, if it pleases your ladyship, allow these poor men who admitted their misunderstanding be put upon the scale as well but without risk of any penalty. For entertainment's sake at least, if not to see if anything positive is to be found amongst them'.

In the first place, I was greatly confused because, in my misery, the only comfort was that I would not have to undergo the humiliation or have to be lashed out of the scales.

I had no doubt that many of the prisoners would rather have spent ten nights with us in the hall.

But, since the Maiden agreed, that was that and we were untied and sent up one by one. Now, although most of them failed, they were not laughed at or beaten but quietly placed on one side.

My companion was the fifth to go and held out bravely. He was applauded by all, especially the captain who had made the request for us and the Maiden showed him the usual respect.

After him, two more were rapidly dismissed. I was the eighth to step up.

I stepped up, trembling and my companion, sitting in his velvet, smiled kindly at me and the Maiden even smiled a little herself.

I withstood all of the weights. The Maiden even commanded the men to draw me up by force. Three men also hung from the other side of the beam but nothing could move me.

One of the pages stood out and shouted at the top of his voice 'That's him!' and the other replied 'Then let him be freed!' and the Maiden gave her approval.

I was received with due ceremony and was given the choice to release one of the prisoners; whoever I pleased. I did not have to think about it for very long and chose the first emperor whom I had pitied. He was immediately set free and respectfully seated with us.

Meanwhile, the last man had been set up and the weights had proved too heavy for him. The Maiden noticed the roses that I had taken from my hat, which I now held in my hands. She sent her page to ask politely if she could have them. I happily sent them to her.

And so, this first act was all finished at around ten in the morning. The trumpets began to sound again although we still could not see them. The bands stood to one side with their prisoners to await the judgement.

A council of the five captains and us was set up and the business submitted by the Maiden, acting as President. She wanted each one to give their opinion of how the prisoners should be dealt with.

The first opinion was that they should all be executed, some more severely than others; namely the ones who had arrogantly pushed themselves forward against the express conditions. Others wanted them to be kept as prisoners.

Neither idea pleased the President or me.

Eventually, one of the emperors (the same one I had freed) together with my companion and I, put forward this proposal:

That the principal lords be led respectfully from the castle, then the others, with less dignity.

Others would be stripped and made to run out naked.

A fourth group would be chased out with rods, whips or dogs.

Those who had willingly surrendered on the previous day would be allowed to leave without blame.

Last of all, the arrogant ones and those who behaved so appallingly at the previous day's dinner, should be punished both in body and life according to the severity of their offence.

This proposal pleased the Maiden very much and was soon carried.

They were also granted another meal, of which they were soon informed but the sentencing was put back to twelve noon.

At this, the senate arose and the Maiden, together with her attendants, returned to her usual place. But the top table in the room was reserved for us and we were requested to wait there until the business was taken care of.

Then, we would be taken to the Lord Bridegroom and Bride. We were all very happy with this.

Meanwhile, the prisoners were brought back into the hall and each man was seated according to his status. They were told to behave in a more civil manner than they had done the day before. However, this instruction was not needed, as they were already subdued and silent.

And I can confidently say, not to flatter but simply being honest, that typically, those people who were of the highest rank knew how to conduct themselves even during their unexpected setback.

They were treated ordinarily and respectfully but still could not see their attendants. We, however, could now see them, which made me incredibly cheerful.

Although fortune had raised us, we did not lord it over the others and advised them to be in good spirits as things would not be so bad for them. Although, they would have really wanted us to tell them their sentence, we were under a strict obligation and none of us dared to open our mouths about it.

However, we comforted them as much as we could and drank with them to see if the wine might cheer them up.

Our table had been covered with red velvet and set out with drinking cups of pure silver and gold. The others viewed this with amazement and no small amount of torment.

Before we were seated, the two pages came in and, on behalf of the Bridegroom, presented everyone a Golden Fleece with a flying lion, asking us to wear these at the table. We were instructed to uphold the reputation and dignity of the order, which had been granted to us by his majesty and would soon be made official with suitable ceremonies.

We accepted this with total compliance and promised faithfully to do whatever his majesty wished of us.

The noble page also had a seating plan and placed us in order. For my part, I will not tell you where they placed me in case this is mistaken as pride, which goes against the fourth weight.

Because we had such an abundance of riches at our table, we asked one of the pages if we were permitted to send some choice pieces to our friends and acquaintances. He said that it was not a problem and each of us sent plenty to his acquaintances via the waiters. As they did not see the waiters and did not know where it would have come from, I went to take some over to them myself. But, as soon as I stood up, one of the waiters was straight at my side. He said that it was just a friendly warning but if one of the pages saw me doing this, he would inform the king, who would not be pleased. He reassured me that, as no one else had seen, he would not tell on me but I must show more respect for the dignity of the order in future.

The servant's words quite took me aback and I hardly moved in my seat for a long time afterwards. I managed to thank him gratefully for his loyal warning, despite my sudden fear.

Soon after, the trumpets sang again. We were used to this now and knew that it was the Maiden, so we stood to receive her. She entered with her usual parade on her high seat with one of the pages in front bearing a very tall gold goblet and the other with a document of parchment.

Having alighted from the seat with wonderful grace, she took the goblet from the page and held it up on the king's behalf saying that it came from his majesty. In honour of him, we must pass it around. On the outside of the goblet was a figure of Fortune, cast in gold, with a red flying ensign in her hand. Because of this, I drank from it, a little unhappily, as I was all too well aware of Fortune's contrariness.

The Maiden was, like us, wearing the Golden Fleece and lion and I thought that she might be the President of the Order. So we asked her the name of the order and she replied that it was not time to reveal this and we must wait until the prisoners were dealt with. Then they were blindfolded. What had already happened to us seemed to them to be mild. And nothing, when compared to the honour we had subsequently been given. They probably had hopes of similar honour.

She took the document from the other page and separated it into two parts, reading this from one part before the first company:

'Now, you should all confess that you have given too much credit to false and fraudulent books. You have assumed too much and have come into this castle uninvited. For the most part putting yourselves forward thinking you would make your names here and afterwards live in pride and grandeur. And so, each one of you has seduced another one and dropped them into disgrace and humiliation, therefore deserving to be soundly punished'.

They humbly accepted this and gave their hands to show this. After this, a severe charge was made to the rest:

'It is declared that you knew quite well, as your consciences are aware, that you have forged fraudulent and false books, have fooled and cheated others and, by doing so, have brought royal dignity into disrepute. Also, that you knowingly made use of ungodly and deceitful figures, not even sparing the divine trinity in your efforts to cheat people all over the country. It is now as clear as day what you have done to trap the true guests and bring in the ignorant. Conducting yourselves in such a manner as to show to the whole world that you have openly indulged in promiscuity, adultery, gluttony and other sins. All of which is against the express orders of our kingdom.

In brief, you knew full well that you belittled his majesty, even amongst the common people. Therefore, you should confess yourselves to be clearly guilty dishonest, cheating, good-for-nothings who deserve to be kept away from polite society and severely punished'.

The good artists were reluctant to make this confession to such an extent that the Maiden herself threatened them and swore that they would die whilst the other company angrily shouted at them that they had wickedly lured them from the light. Eventually, to prevent total disaster, they confessed with sadness but in addition claimed that what had happened here should not be totally blamed upon them considering that the lords, being absolutely determined to get into the castle, had promised them great sums of money to do so. So each of them had used every trick in the book until they had all ended up in this situation. 'Just because it hadn't succeeded, the lords were no less guilty and they shouldn't be treated any differently. Who would have thought that, if anyone took the chance of getting in by climbing the wall with them, that there would be so much danger for so little an advantage?'

Also, they claimed that their books sold so well that anyone with no other means to maintain a standard of living had no choice but to take part in the deception. They also hoped that, if justice was done, they would be found completely innocent as they had only served the lords by giving them what they wanted.

In reply, they were told that his royal majesty had resolved to punish them all, every man. Some more severely than others.

For, although what they had alleged was partly true and because of this the lords should not be let off lightly, there were still good reasons that they should still prepare themselves for death. They had acted deliberately and maliciously and coerced the ignorant against their will. And the same could be said of those who had degraded his royal majesty with their false writings and books.

On hearing this, many of them began to weep and wail pitifully, begging and prostrating themselves pathetically. All of which made no difference.

I was astonished that the Maiden could remain so resolute when just seeing their misery caused us to weep and pity them (despite most of them having given us nothing but trouble).

She dispatched her page who brought in all of the soldiers [66] who had been on duty at the scales. They were ordered to collect their prisoners and form an orderly procession to take them to her great garden. I was amazed when each one of them instantly recognized their prisoner and went directly to him.

My companions and I were given permission to go into the garden, unbound, to be present at the execution of the sentence.

As soon as we had all come forward, the Maiden mounted her high throne and asked us all to sit upon the steps and attend the judgement. We obeyed, leaving everything standing on the table (except the goblet, which the Maiden gave to one of the pages for safekeeping). We went forward in our robes on the throne, which moved as if it were floating on air. In this way, we entered the garden, where we all stood.

The garden was not particularly unusual and I was pleased to see the trees planted so neatly. There was also a magnificent fountain, decorated with beautiful figures and inscriptions and strange symbols (which, God willing, I will detail in a future book).

A wooden scaffold was erected in the garden. It had coverlets around it, which were decorated with painted figures.

Four galleries were built, one on top of the other. The first was the most impressive and was covered with a white taffeta curtain so we could not see who sat in it. The second was undecorated and empty. The last two were covered with red and blue taffeta.

As soon as we came to the scaffold, the Maiden bowed to the ground and we were very frightened as we guessed that the King and Queen would not be far away. We duly bowed in the same manner and the Maiden led us up the winding stairs, into the second gallery and sat uppermost with us arranged as before.

How the emperor I had freed behaved towards me, here and at the table, I will not say, as to do so would invite idle gossip. But he doubtless imagined how tormented and concerned he would have been if he was now shamefully awaiting judgement instead of having gained such dignity and worthiness due to my intervention.

And now the Maiden who had originally brought me the invitation and, until now, I had not seen since, entered. First, she gave one blast on her trumpet and in a thundering voice, read out the sentence:

'The king's majesty, my most gracious lord, wishes with all his heart that each and every person assembled here had, upon his majesty's invitation, presented themselves as suitable and to have honoured him by attending his appointed wedding and joyful feast. But, since Almighty God has seen fit to make it otherwise, his majesty has no complaint but is forced, against his own inclination, to abide by the ancient and worthy constitutions of this kingdom.

However, so his majesty's natural mercifulness may be seen throughout the world, he has negotiated with his council and estates to significantly reduce the usual sentence.

Therefore, in the first place he is willing to spare the lives of the lords and rulers and directly release them. He wishes them to know that they should not take it badly that they will not be present at his majesty's feast of honour but to remember that God Almighty expects much more of you and he alone decides how to distribute his gifts.

Nor has your reputation been tarnished, although you are still rejected by our order as we cannot do everything at once.

And as for you having been captivated by lowlife crooks: they will not go unpunished.

Furthermore, his majesty promises shortly to send you an 'Index Expurgatorius' or 'Catalogue of Heretics' or 'Deletion List'[67] so you may be able to better judge the differences between good and evil in future.

As his majesty intends to sort through his library and offer any seductive writings to Vulcan (by burning them), he asks you politely and humbly to do the same, with the hope that all evil and mischief may be stopped for the time being. In addition, you are urged to never so thoughtlessly seek entrance again, as your excuse of having been seduced will not work and you will fall in disgrace and be held in contempt by all men.

Finally, as much as the estates of the land still have something to demand from your lordships, his majesty hopes that none of you will mind redeeming yourselves by giving a chain or anything else you have about you so we can part as friends and we will make sure you get home safely.

Those who did not stand up to the first, third or fourth weight will not be so lightly dismissed by his majesty. But, to show his majesty's mercy to you, you will be stripped naked and dismissed.

Those who were found too light for the second and fifth weight shall, in addition to being stripped, be branded with one, two or more marks according to which one was lighter or heavier.

Those who were drawn up by the sixth or seventh and not by the others will be dealt with more kindly and should step forward. (A particular punishment was given, depending on each combination but it is too long to repeat here).

Those who stood aside of their own accord yesterday will go freely and without blame.

Finally, the convicted travelling cheats who could not move any of the weights, shall be punished in body and life with the sword, rope, water and rods. And such execution of judgement should be clearly seen as an example to others'.

On this, our Maiden broke her staff and the other, who had read out the sentence, blew her trumpet and stepped with great reverence towards those standing behind the curtain.

At this point, I must not forget to tell you about the number of prisoners; There were seven of those who weighed one, twenty-one of those who weighed two, thirty-five weighed three, thirty-five weighed four, twenty-one weighed five and seven weighed six. But the only one that got to the seventh but could not raise it was the same man whom I released.

Apart from these, there were many who totally failed. And not many who drew all of the weights from the ground. As each stood before us, I carefully numbered them and wrote it in my notebook.

In addition, it is very commendable that amongst all those that weighed anything, none of them were equal to any other. Although there were thirty-five of those who weighed three, only one weighed the first second and third. Another weighed the third, fourth and fifth. Another, the fifth, sixth and seventh and so on.

It is equally wonderful that, amongst one hundred and twenty-six who weighed anything, that none was equal to another. I would willingly name them all together with each man's weight but time does not allow. I hope it will be published later, with the interpretation.

With the judgement having been read, the lords in the first place, were very satisfied as it was such a severe situation they did not expect a light sentence.

So they gave generously and more than was expected of them. Each one redeemed himself with chains, jewels, gold, money and other items, as much as they had on them and with respect, left us.

The king's servants were forbidden to laugh but some were unable to stifle their giggles, as it was funny to see them pack up so hastily and rush off without once looking behind them.

Some of them asked if the catalogue could be sent to them immediately so they could get to work on sorting out their books as his majesty wished. They were assured that they would receive copies.

As they got to the door, each one was given a drink from a cup containing a potion of forgetfulness[68] so they would not remember their misfortune.

After they had gone, the ones who had stood aside also left. They were allowed to pass freely and were told that they would be welcomed back if they came better prepared next time.

Meanwhile, others were being stripped and treated according to their sins; some were just sent away naked but untouched, others with small bells attached and some were whipped as they left.

There were so many different punishments carried out that I cannot remember them all.

In the end, it was time to deal with the final group. This took some time as some were hanged, some beheaded, some forced into the water and drowned and other various methods of execution.

I wept at the sight of the executions. Not because of the punishment, which they totally deserved but at the thought of human blindness and our continual meddling with things that have been forbidden to us ever since the first fall of man.

And so the garden, which until recently was full, became almost empty. Besides the soldiers, there was not a single person left.

As soon as it was all done, there was a five-minute silence. Then, a beautiful snow-white unicorn came in with a golden collar around its neck (which had certain letters on it).

He bowed down with his front legs as if showing respect for the lion that stood on the fountain. It had been so still that I'd assumed it was a stone or brass statue but the lion then took the sword it held in its claws and broke it into two, the pieces sinking into the fountain. He then roared for a long time until a white dove, bearing an olive branch in her beak, flew in and was immediately eaten by the lion, who was instantly calm. The unicorn happily returned to its place.

Our Maiden led us from the scaffold and down the winding stairs and we bowed towards the curtain.

We were told to wash our hands and faces in the fountain and to wait for a little while until the King had gone back to his hall using a secret passageway.

We were then escorted back to our room with fine music, much ceremony and cheerful conversation. This was all completed by around four in the afternoon.

In order to pass the time, the Maiden assigned a noble page to each one of us. They were not only richly dressed but exceptionally well-educated and could talk informedly on so many topics that we were put to shame.

The pages had been instructed to take us on tours of the castle (but only in certain areas) and see to our requests, where possible.

The Maiden then left us, saying that it would not be long before we saw her again at supper. After that we would celebrate with the ceremony of hanging up the weights[69]. She added that we should remain patient as tomorrow, we would be presented to the King.

After she had gone, each of us did whatever he felt like doing.

Some went to look at the excellent paintings and sketched copies for themselves, thinking about the meaning of the wonderful symbolism in each.

Others were happy to have some more food and drink.

I asked my page to take my companion and me around the castle. I will never regret that decision as long as I live!

As well the wonderful antiquities, we were shown the royal crypt and learned more than we ever could from books.

In that place stood the glorious phoenix (I had written a short article about this two years ago). I am now determined (in case it proves useful) to write more about the lion, eagle, griffin, falcon and so on, with illustrations and explanations of their inscriptions.

I feel sorry for my other companions as they missed out on such precious treasures. And yet, I cannot help but think that it was God's will.

I made the most of my page. Each of them was gifted in being able to direct each person to the rooms and places that they would most enjoy.

The keys belonging to the royal crypt had already been given to my page so I was lucky to get first choice. But, although he invited others to come along, they imagined there was not much to see and thought that all the interesting tombs would be in the churchyard.

Regardless, my companion and I have sketched the monuments and copied the inscriptions so they can be made available to any interested academic.

The other thing we got to see was the library, preserved just as it was before the reformation. Just the thought of it gladdens my heart but I will not go into great detail, as the catalogue of it will soon be published.

At the entrance to it stands an enormous book, the like of which I had never before seen. It recorded all of the figures, rooms and doorways in the castle as well as all the writing, riddles and so on.

Now, I know that I made a promise regarding this but I must restrain myself and learn more about the world first.

Inside every book was a picture of the author. Many of these would be burned so that any memory of them would be forgotten by the good.

Having seen all of this but barely having left the library, another page came running towards us and to our page. He urgently whispered something to him, in response to which, he handed over the keys, which the other page immediately took with him up the winding stairs.

Our page was left standing there, looking quite shaken. We urged him to tell us what had happened. He eventually replied that he had been informed that the king's majesty had said that neither the library nor the crypt were to be seen by any man and were absolutely forbidden. He begged us not to tell anyone as he had already said to the other page that we had not gone in either. It would cost him his life if it was discovered that we had.

Both of us alternated between joy and fear after this but fortunately, nobody enquired any further about it. We had spent three hours exploring both places, which I do not regret at all.

It was past seven o'clock and, so far, we had not had anything to eat. However, we easily forgot our hunger as we were continually uplifted and I felt almost as if I could happily fast for the rest of my life with so many interesting distractions.

We were shown fountains, mines, art and craft workshops and each one of them was far superior to all of our own rolled into one. All of the rooms were built in a semi-circle so everyone could see the expensive and magnificent clockwork orrery and carry out their work according to the position of the planets, which were seen upon it.

I could easily see where our own artists failed but it is not up to me to tell them.

Eventually, I entered a large room (which the others had been shown before). In the middle of the room was a globe of the Earth, thirty feet in diameter. Almost half of it, except for the steps leading up to it was recessed into the floor. In this way, it could be easily spun about by two men but half of it would always be out of view and you would only be able to see the parts that were above the horizon.

It was obvious that this had been made for a special purpose but I could not work out what the gold rings I could see in several places were for. I asked my page and he laughed and said 'Look closer'. I looked at the globe and spotted my home country circled by one of the rings. My companion came over and saw that his homeland was marked in the same way. All of the others came and looked and each one found that gold rings marked their countries too. The page said that only yesterday their astronomer (they called him 'Old Atlas') told the king that the gold rings had been set to mark everyone's home country. The pages had noticed that there was a mark on my homeland but no one chosen to account for it. He guessed that I had underrated myself and got one of the captains to request that we should also be put upon the scales without fear of penalty. This was also the reason why he, the most powerful of the pages, was personally assigned to me.

I thanked him profusely and looked more carefully at my native country on the globe. As well as the ring surrounding it, there were fine lines on it too. I do not want to be thought of as showing off about it though.

There was a lot more to the globe than I am willing to share but think about this: Why doesn't every town on Earth produce a philosopher?

After this, we were taken right inside the globe by means of a large square trapdoor built in the sea. There was a tablet with the artist's name and three dedications inscribed on it; by lifting it you could open the trapdoor and walk over a board to get inside the globe. The centre just had a round board, which could comfortably seat four people. Even in broad daylight (it was dark at this time), you could come here and study the stars.

To my mind, they were glittering gems, which sparkled beautifully and moved so elegantly that I did not want to leave. I could have stayed there forever. The page told the Maiden about this later and she often teased me about it!

However, it was already time for supper. I had spent so long in the globe that I was almost the last to sit down so I didn't hang about but put on my gown again (I had laid it aside beforehand) and went straight to the table. The waiters treated me with so much respect and admiration that I lowered my head in embarrassment. Because of this I did not notice until it was too late, that the Maiden was on one side of me and had stood as I approached. She noticed my discomfort, so took hold of my gown and led me to the table.

It is a waste of time trying to express how wonderful the music and other entertainment was. I simply do not have words to do it justice. In a nutshell, there was nothing but art and pleasure.

We all chatted about our day since noon (but not mentioning the library or crypt of course) and were quite getting quite merry with all the wine when the Maiden put this to us:

'My lords, I have a disagreement with one of my sisters. In our room, we have an eagle. We love him and both make a fuss of him and want to be his favourite. On that score, we have had plenty of rows about it. One day we decided that we would go over to him together and whichever one of us he was most friendly to would have him. This we did and I, as usual, carried a branch of laurel in my hand. When he saw us, he gave the branch he had in his beak to my sister then immediately took my laurel from my hand. After this, both of us thought that he had liked us best. So, how do we resolve it?'

It pleased us very much that she had asked our opinion and I think that every one of us would have liked to hear a good answer to the puzzle. But they were all looking at me and clearly expecting me to go first. I was pretty much stumped so I asked her a question instead:

'Gracious Lady, your problem would be easily solved but one thing puzzles me: I once had two friends who loved me a great deal. They could not decide which one of them I liked best so, without my knowing, they decided to both run to me and whichever one I hugged first would be my favourite. They did this but one could not keep up with the other so he stopped, crying as the other one got to me first and, although I was a bit startled, hugged him.

Later, they told me about it and I did not know what to say to them to resolve it either. I have had to leave it until I get some good advice myself.'

The Maiden thought about it and understood my position. She said 'Well, let us both give up and we'll get the answer from the others'

However, they had realised what I had done and how to answer, so the next one said:

'In the city I live in, a maiden was condemned to death. The judge was sympathetic though and said that if anyone would champion her, he should come forward freely. She had two lovers and one of them came forward into the enclosure to face his opponent. Then, the other came forward but he was obviously too late. Despite this, he insisted on fighting as her champion's opponent. When the fight began, he deliberately allowed himself to be beaten so that the maiden could go free.

So, tell me my lords, which one should get the girl?'

The Maiden could not keep quiet any longer. She said 'I was hoping to get some advice but I see I have got myself trapped! Nethertheless, I will gladly hear more if anyone wants to tell me another'.

'Yes, indeed!' answered a third 'And a stranger tale you will not hear: When I was younger, I loved a worthy woman and in order to seduce her, I used the services of an old woman who brought us together. The three of us were together when suddenly, the girl's brothers came in and went absolutely crazy, threatening to kill me! I begged and begged them not to do so and finally they calmed down. However, they forced me to swear that I would marry BOTH of the women for one year each!

So tell me, my lords – should I have the old one or the young one first..?'

We all roared with laughter at this but, although a few of us muttered to each other about it, no one attempted to answer the riddle.

Then, a fourth one started off:

'In a city, which shall remain nameless, there lived an honourable married lady. She was loved by many but especially by a young nobleman. However, he was far too persistent until finally she said to him that, if he got her into a pretty green and warm garden of roses in the middle of a cold winter then he could have her. But if not, he was to leave her alone for good.

The nobleman travelled all over the world to find someone who could do this for him. Finally, he came across an old man who promised to do if he gave him half of his estate as payment. He agreed to this and the old man was as good as his word. The nobleman invited the lady to his garden. To her surprise, she found that it was warm, pretty, lush and green. She remembered her promise and asked only to return to her husband one last time. With sighs and tears, she told her husband about the terrible mess she was in. The husband could see that she had tried to be faithful to him but sent her back to the lover who had spent a fortune to get her, to enable her to honour the deal she had made. The nobleman was so touched by the integrity of the husband's actions that he considered it would be sinful to touch such an honest wife and, with the deepest respect, sent her back home to her husband. In turn, the old man felt, regardless of how poor he was, that he could not be any less honourable than the other men. He gave back everything the nobleman had paid him and went on his way.

Now my lords – Which of these persons do you think showed the most virtue?'

We fell silent. The Maiden made no response other than calling for anyone else who wanted to contribute.

And so, the fifth speaker began:

'My lords, I will keep this short: Who has the greater love? He who sees what he loves or he who only thinks about it?'

'He who sees it' answered the Maiden.

'No' I responded.

A debate started about this, so a sixth person shouted out:

'My lords, I am getting married. I can choose from a maid, a married woman or a widow. Help me choose and I will sort the rest out'.

'That's all very well,' replied the seventh 'if you *have* a choice but as for me, I don't. When I was young, I loved a beautiful and good maiden. I loved her from the bottom of my heart and she felt the same way. But her friends opposed it and we could not marry. So, later on she married someone else; a decent and honest man who treated her well, loved and supported her. She was pregnant and when time came to give birth it went very badly and everyone thought she was dead. She was buried with dignity and greatly mourned.

I thought to myself 'You could not have her when she was alive but now she is dead you can hold and kiss her to your heart's content'.

I took my servant with me and got him to dig her up. I opened the coffin and held her in my arms. I suddenly felt some faint movement in her heart, which increased with the warmth from my body as I touched her. Finally, I saw that she really was still alive.

I quietly took her back to my home and warmed her in a bath of expensive herbs. I left her with my mother until she gave birth to a healthy boy. I provided a nurse for the boy as well as his mother.

Two days later, when she had sufficiently recovered, I explained what had happened. I asked her to live with me as my wife but she refused, as it would be a terrible thing to do to her husband, who had treated her well and looked after her. However, she did admit that as far as love went she owed me, as well as him.

Two months later (as I got ready to go on a trip), I invited her husband over as a guest. During our conversation, I asked him if his dead wife were to return, would he be happy to take her back? With tears in his eyes and much sobbing, he said that he would.

At this point, I brought out his wife and son and told him everything that had happened. I then begged him to give her up and consent to me marrying her instead. We argued long and hard about it but, in the end, he could not deny that I had a claim on his wife but we could not agree about the son'.

The Maiden interrupted 'How on earth could you put that poor man through this for a second time?!'

'What?' he replied 'Do you think I wasn't bothered?'

A fierce argument broke out at this point although most of us said that he was in the right.

'No!' he said 'I let him have his wife and son back in the end. Now, tell me my lords, which was greater; my honesty or the other man's joy?'

The Maiden was so happy to hear this that she proposed a toast.

There were other tales thrown in after this but they were so confusing that I cannot remember all of them. However, one of them does spring to mind: One man said that a few years ago he had seen a doctor who bought a bundle of wood for winter. All winter long, it kept him warm but, when the spring came, he sold the very same wood again, and so he had been warmed for free.

'That takes some doing' said the Maiden 'but we've gone on long enough'.

'Yes' my companion replied 'If anyone can't work out the answers to any of the riddles, they should let the speaker know through a messenger and get the answer that way'.

At this point, we returned thanks to God and got up from the table satisfied and merry, rather than full. I wish that all occasions and dinners could be like this.

After wandering around the hall a little, the Maiden asked us is we wanted to start the wedding.

'Yes, my good lady' said one.

She signalled to a page and remained chatting to us. I felt so close to her already that I actually asked her name. She smiled at this but did not seem bothered by it and replied:

'My name contains five and fifty, and yet has only eight letters; the third letter is a third of the fifth, which added to the sixth produces a number whose root is greater than the third by just the value of the first, and it is also half of the fourth. Now the fifth and the seventh are equal, the last and the first are also equal, and when added to the second is as much as the sixth, which equals four more than the third tripled. Now tell me, my lord, what am I called?'

That was complicated enough but I didn't give up and said to her
 'Noble and virtuous lady, can you tell me just one letter?'
 'Yes, alright' she said
 'What is the seventh letter?'
 'It is as many as there are lords here'
I was happy with this and was easily able to work it out[70]. She was very pleased that I had and said that much more would be revealed to us.

In the meantime, some of the maidens had prepared themselves and now entered in a grand parade. First came two youths carrying lights. One looked very cheerful with bright eyes and good looks, the other just looked aggressive (I later discovered that whatever he wanted, he got).

Next came four maidens. One bowed her head demurely and was very unassuming in her manner. The second appeared shy and reserved too.

As the third maiden entered, she seemed startled. I found out that she felt uncomfortable at festive occasions.

The fourth showed her kindness and generosity by bringing small bunches of flowers.

After these four came two more who were even more finely dressed. They politely bowed to us. One had a dress of blue, which sparkled with golden stars. The other was wearing a green dress, decorated with red and white stripes. They wore light, flowing scarves on their heads, which really suited them.

Finally, there entered one with a coronet on her head. She looked up towards heaven and we all thought that this must be the Bride, but we were wrong. Although, in fairness, she was actually more finely and richly dressed than the Bride and was even more important. Afterwards, she presided over the entire wedding.

Our Maiden knelt before her so we did the same. However, she was extremely humble and offered her hand to each person telling us not to make a fuss as it was the least she could do for us. She told us to look to our creator and accept that he was all-powerful and then to go about our lives and use this honour to praise God and benefit mankind.

Briefly, her words were quite different from those of our Maiden, who was much worldlier. They really got under my skin.

'And you,' she said, turning to me, 'have received more than others, make sure that you also give more back.'

It seemed to be quite a strange speech. When we first saw the maidens and heard the music we thought that there would be dancing but that had not happened.

The weights that I previously mentioned were still in the same place so the maiden with the coronet (who later turned out to be the

Queen[71]) commanded each maiden to take one and follow her. The last and heaviest weight was her own. She assigned this to our Maiden, who took it easily.

Our own importance felt somewhat diminished, as it was obvious that our Maiden was far too good for us. We felt that we were nowhere near as important as we might have imagined.

So, we followed the procession and were brought into the first room where our Maiden, who was at the front, hung up the Queen's weight. During this, an excellent and spiritual hymn was sung. There was nothing extravagant in this room, just a set of little prayer books (which should always be available).

The Queen knelt at a pulpit in the centre of the room. We all knelt around her and repeated a prayer read from a book. The prayer asked that the wedding would be to the honour of God and to benefit ourselves.

Afterwards, we entered the second room in the same manner, our Maiden hanging up her weight once again. And so it continued until all the ceremonies had finished. The Queen once again offered her hand to everyone and left with her maidens.

Our own President (our Maiden) remained with us for a while. It was two o'clock at night though and she clearly did not want to keep us up. She seemed a little reluctant to leave us, probably because she was enjoying our company, but she said goodnight and wished us all a good night's sleep before leaving us.

Our pages were very well organised and took each of us to his room. There was another bed in each room, where they slept, so we could easily call them if we needed anything. My room (I have no idea what the others were like) was grandly decorated with fine tapestries and paintings. Above all else though, I most enjoyed spending time with my page, who was so well-spoken and knowledgeable that I spent a further hour just talking with him. It was half past three when I finally fell asleep. This was the first chance I had to get a decent night's sleep and yet, I was disturbed by a bad dream! I kept dreaming about a door that I could not open but eventually managed to. I had these dreams right through the night until I woke up close to dawn.

CHAPTER THREE: NOTES

[66] The soldiers are specifically described here as 'Kurrisers' who were armed cavalry units similar to the Late Medieval 'man-at-arms'. They wore three-quarter armour protecting the upper body and front of the legs. The breastplate was called a cuirass (in French) which gave rise to the name 'cuirassier' and 'Kurriser' in German.

[67] The lists are given in Latin as a *'Catalogum haereticorum'* (Catalogue of Heretics) or *'Index Expurgatorius'* (Deletion List).

Later in the 16th century, the Catholic Church published the *'Index Librorum Prohibitorum'* (List of Prohibited Books) which later included an *'Index Expurgatorius'* of works that were deemed worthy if certain parts of them were removed. ('Banned book lists' by the Catholic Church had existed since the 9th century but were not officially authorized).

[68] *Oblivionis haustus* (Forgetfulness draught) in the original text

[69] *Suspensionis ponderu (Weights suspension)* ceremony in the original text.

[70] **The Name of the Maiden**
'My name contains five and fifty, and yet has only eight letters; the third letter is a third of the fifth, which added to the sixth produces a number whose root is greater than the third by just the value of the first, and it is also half of the fourth. Now the fifth and the seventh are equal, the last and the first are also equal, and when added to the second is as much as the sixth, which equals four more than the third tripled. Now tell me, my lord, what am I called?'

'What is the seventh letter?'
'It is as many as there are lords here'

Here we go...

We set out eight letters
‑ ‑ ‑ ‑ ‑ ‑ ‑ ‑

If we assume a substitution cipher of numbers for letters, which does seem to be implied, the number of lords and therefore the seventh letter cannot exceed 26. It also has to be divisible by three because we are told that letters 7 and 5 have an equal value and that the third letter is a third of the fifth. So we can have the following values for 7 (and 5); 3(C),6(F),9(I),12(L),15(O),18(R),21(U),24(X)

```
_ _ _ _ _ C _ C _
_ _ _ _ _ F _ F _
_ _ _ _ _ I _ I _
_ _ _ _ _ L _ L _
_ _ _ _ _ O _ O _
_ _ _ _ _ R _ R _
_ _ _ _ _ U _ U _
_ _ _ _ _ X _ X _
```

The third letter is a third of the fifth. For the first example line C=3 so a third of this would be 1, or A:

```
_ _ A _ C _ C _
_ _ B _ F _ F _
_ _ C _ I _ I _
_ _ D _ L _ L _
_ _ E _ O _ O _
_ _ F _ R _ R _
_ _ G _ U _ U _
_ _ H _ X _ X _
```

The sixth letter is the value of the third x 3 and plus 4
So the first line would be A=1 x 3 = 3. Plus 4 =7 or G. As we exceed 26, we lose the last line

```
_ _ A _ C G C _
_ _ B _ F J F _
_ _ C _ I M I _
_ _ D _ L P L _
_ _ E _ O S O _
_ _ F _ R V R _
_ _ G _ U Y U _
```

We can eliminate the first two lines too due to CGC and FJF being an unlikely part of any name. Now, a third of the fifth value, added to the sixth (which we now know) produces a number – let's work that out first for each row

```
_ _ C _ I M I _ 3+13 = 16
_ _ D _ L P L _ 4+16=20
_ _ E _ O S O _ 5+19=24
_ _ F _ R V R _ 6+22=28
_ _ G _ U Y U _ 7+25=32
```

The root of this number is half of the fourth but the only 'clean' root we can use is 16 on our new first line…

_ _ C H I M I _ (4x2=8 or H)

This root (4) was greater than the third (C=3) by the value of the first letter, which must be 1 (4 -3) or A. In addition, the first and eight letters are the same:

A _ C H I M I A

One to go…
The value of the last (or first), which is 1, plus the second letter equals the value of the sixth (M=13). Or sixth (13) minus last (1) equals the second which will be 12 or L
So the name is:
ALCHIMIA

[71] Some translations describe this lady as 'The Duchess'. The German word used is Königin: literally 'Queen'.

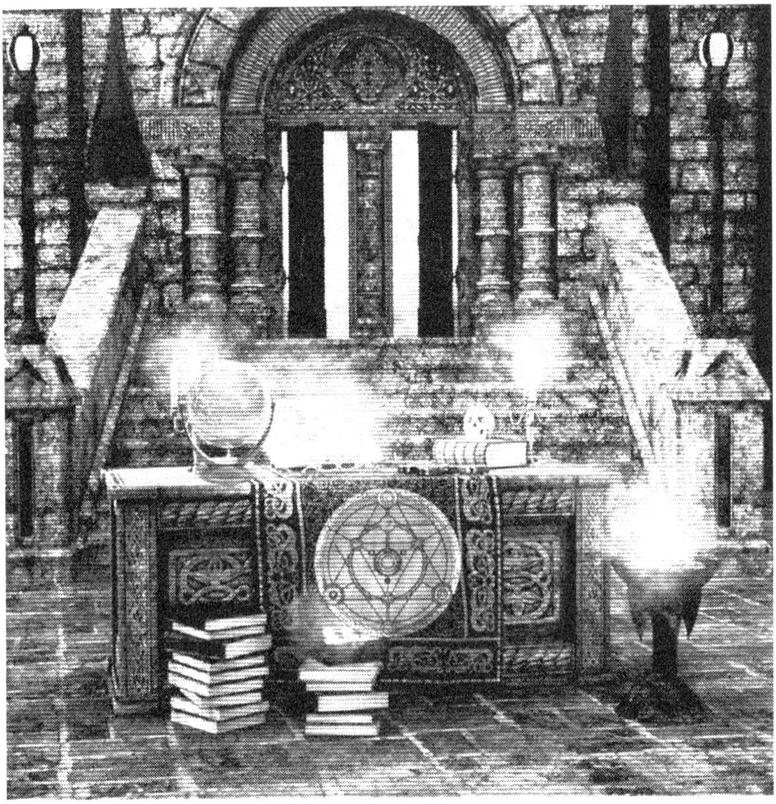

Chapter Four

The Fourth Day

I was lying in bed and casually looking at all of the paintings and tapestries in my chamber when there came the sound of horns playing as if a procession was in progress. My page immediately leapt out of bed, shocked and looking like death warmed up.

You can imagine my reaction when he said 'The others are already being presented to the king!'. I was gutted and did not know what to do, other than to curse my own laziness and to get dressed. My page was way ahead of me and ran out of the bedroom to see what the situation was.

He soon returned and luckily, had some good news. It was not time to meet the King just yet and we had only missed the call for breakfast. They had been reluctant to wake me because of my age so had allowed me to sleep in.

Now it was time and the Page would take me to a fountain where most of the others were already gathered. I cheered up immensely on hearing this and quickly got ready. We returned to the garden and the Maiden made fun of me for having such a long lie-in! When we got to the fountain, we saw the Lion, who now had a large tablet instead of his sword.

Reading it, I discovered that it had been removed from the ancient monuments and placed here for some special purpose. As the inscription was rather worn and difficult to read, I will set it out here so everyone has the chance to read it:

'Hermes the prince.
After mankind has been so wounded
By the grace of God and the assistance of art
I flow here as a healing medicine.

Let he who can, drink me,
Wash in me if you wish,
Disturb me if you dare,
Drink Brothers and live!'[72]

It is a good idea to read and understand this inscription and it is appropriate for me to put it here, as it is the easiest one to understand.

We all washed ourselves at the fountain and drank from it using a cup of pure gold. We were then instructed to follow the Maiden to the hall and change into new clothes, which were made from a golden cloth and beautifully decorated with flowers. We all received another Golden

Fleece, set with precious stones and decorations made by the finest craftsmen. On the fleece hung a heavy gold medal. On one side was the sun and moon facing each other. The other side bore an inscription reading 'The light of the moon shall be as bright as the sun, and the light of the sun shall be seven times brighter than it is now.'

The jewels we had had before were collected and placed in a little casket. One of the servants took this away.

After this, the Maiden led us in procession to the musicians, who were waiting at the door and dressed in red velvet with white belts. A door (which I had not seen opened before) was unlocked, revealing the royal winding staircase. Accompanied by music, the Maiden led us up the three hundred and sixty-five steps. Everything along the way was amazingly detailed and expensive and, the further we climbed, the more magnificent the decorations. When we gained the summit of the winding staircase we arrived at a painted arched vault[73] where the sixty maidens, all finely dressed, joined us.

They bowed to us and we returned the greeting. The musicians were sent away and descended the staircase. The door at the bottom was closed after them.

Then, a little bell chimed and a beautiful maiden came in and handed us all wreaths of laurel and branches of laurel for the other maidens.

A curtain was drawn up and I saw the King and Queen in all their glory. If the Queen had not strictly warned me the day before, I might have forgotten myself and thought that this was as magnificent as heaven itself.

Apart from the fact that the room glittered with gold and precious stones, the Queen's robes were beautiful beyond my comprehension. If I had thought anything before this was beautiful; well, this was as far above everything else I had seen as the stars are in the heavens.

Meanwhile, the Maiden entered and each of the other maidens took one of us by the hand and with the greatest dignity and respect, presented each of us in turn to the King.

The Maiden began to speak:

'In honour of your royal majesties, our most gracious King and Queen, these lords here present have travelled here, risking life and limb. Your majesties will be pleased to learn that nearly all of them are highly qualified to increase your estates and empire, as you will surely agree if you were to examine them closely.

I therefore wish to have them presented to your majesties and most humbly request your permission to step down from my role. I also humbly request that you question them sufficiently to determine whether or not I have fulfilled that role adequately'.

She laid her laurel branch on the ground.

It would probably have been appropriate for one of us to have said something at this point but we were all dumbstruck.

At last, Old Atlas stepped forward and spoke on the King's behalf:

'Their royal majesties are delighted to see you and give their royal blessing to each and every one of you.

Gentle Maiden, they are most grateful and satisfied with your performance and wish to suitably reward you. However, they ask that you continue your duties today, as they are most confident in your abilities'.

On this, the Maiden picked up the branch again. She stepped aside and we did the same.

We came to a rectangular room that was squared at the front and five times longer than its width. In the west was a great archway, similar to a porch. In a circle stood three magnificent thrones, the middle one being higher than the rest. Two people sat on each throne. In the first was a very old king with a grey beard but his consort was young and exceptionally beautiful. In the third throne was a middle-aged black king and, next to him, a delicate old lady who was covered with a veil rather than a crown.

In the middle were two youngsters. They wore laurel wreaths on their heads with a large and expensive crown suspended over them. To be honest, they were actually not as attractive as I had imagined.

Behind them, on a rounded seat, sat mostly elderly men. I was surprised to see that not one of them had a sword or any other weapon. There appeared to be no bodyguards either, although some maidens who had been with us the day before sat on the sides of the arch.

I must tell you about the little Cupid, who flew to and fro! Mostly, he hovered over and around the great crown, sometimes flew down and sat between the two lovers, smiling and teasing them with his tiny bow. Sometimes he cheekily acted as if he was about to shoot one of us! He was so full of fun and mischief and chased the poor little birds that flew in their flocks around the room. The maidens joined in with the fun and whenever they managed to catch him, he had to struggle mightily to get away from them again. And so, this little fellow gave everyone much entertainment and fun.

In front of the Queen was a small and unusual altar, which had on it a book, covered with black velvet and overlaid with gold. There was also a small candle in an ivory candlestick. It was very small but burned continuously. If Cupid hadn't jokingly tried to blow it out every now and again we wouldn't have thought that it was real fire.

Next to this was a celestial globe, which spun around on its own. Next to the globe was a small watch that chimed and then a small crystal pipe or syphon of some sort, which continually ran with a clear blood-red liquid.

Finally, was a skull or 'death's head', which contained a white serpent. She was so long that, as she wound herself around the altar in a circle her tail remained in one of the eye sockets until the head reached the other. Therefore, she was continually in the skull apart from the odd occasion when Cupid came poking at her, in which case she shot completely into the skull at an astonishing speed!

As well as the altar, there were various pictures up and down the room, which moved as if they were alive and had such strange mechanisms as to be beyond my description.

As we paraded out, there was a marvellous choral music. I could not tell if this was coming from the maidens who had stayed behind or from the pictures.

We were more than happy to leave with our maidens and went down the winding stairs. Once again, the door was securely locked behind us.

As soon as we were all in the hall, one of the maidens immediately said 'I'm thinking my sister, that it is a bit risky for you to keep hanging around all of these men'.

'My sister,' our Maiden replied 'The only man that worries me is this one.'

At this, she pointed directly at me. I was quite hurt as she was clearly mocking my age (I was the oldest by far in our group). She noticed this and, to make me feel better, said that, if I played my cards right, she could soon take care of my problem!

A light meal was served and everyone's maiden sat next to him. They were such good company that the time flew by. What they talked and joked about though, is strictly between them and us. I will say that most of the talk was about the arts and both young and old alike were well educated in these topics. However, my mind kept wandering to the Maiden's joke about my age and I kept thinking about being young again which made me a little depressed.

The Maiden noticed this and said out loud 'I'll bet you anything that if I sleep with him tonight, he'll have cheered up by the morning!'

Everyone laughed, including me, although I was blushing bright red.

At this point, one of my Brothers decided to give the Maiden a taste of her own medicine 'Well everyone, you all heard it – our Lady President has promised to sleep with him tonight!'

'I'd be happy to,' said the Maiden 'if I wasn't so afraid of my sisters here. They'd kill me if I picked the best-looking man for myself!'.

'My sister,' one of the maidens replied 'we know that your management position hasn't swollen your head so; if you let us draw lots for the other gentlemen and we can see who we get to sleep with, we're only too happy for you to have first pick'.

We all enjoyed this banter and resumed our conversations. But the Maiden wasn't finished yet.

'My lords,' she said 'how about we let chance decide who sleeps with whom tonight?'

'Well,' I responded 'if that's the offer, how could we refuse?'

As it had been decided to go through with this after the meal and we had now finished, we rose and each man walked up and down with his maiden.

'Ah-ah, not so fast!' said the Maiden 'Split up; we need to see how chance is going to pair us up'.

An argument started over how it was going to be done but this turned out to be an act as the Maiden already had it all worked out:

She proposed that we should all mix ourselves up and stand in a circle. She would count seven from herself and that person would pair up with the one who was seventh down from them, whether it was a man or a woman.

It seemed fair enough so we agreed. We mixed ourselves up randomly (as we thought). However, the maidens were much smarter than we were and each one of them knew exactly where to stand…

The Maiden began to count: the seventh from her was one of the other maidens. Then, the seventh from her was another maiden and the seventh from her, another maiden! And so it continued until, to our amazement, every one of the maidens was paired up with another and not one of us had been chosen!

So, there we were; left standing in a circle looking like idiots whilst the maidens laughed themselves silly at us. We had to admit – we had been totally fooled. No one would have believed it was possible from the order we stood in that none of us would be chosen! Well, that was that and we had to stand there and take it.

Meanwhile, little playful Cupid flew in to the hall. He could not stop to play and instead presented himself on behalf of their royal majesties and brought a golden cup from them so we could drink a toast to health. He had also come to summon our Maiden to the King and could not stay. We thanked him and he flew off again.

Because (in the interim) the mood of my companions had fallen a little (although the maidens weren't too bothered by this!) the maidens started dancing. I did not want to join in and just enjoyed watching, although some of my more flamboyant companions were giving it their all on the dancefloor!

After a few dances our President returned and announced that, before they left, the artists and students would be presenting a play – a merry comedy - in honour of their royal majesties. Their majesties had extended the invitation to anyone who would like to attend and would be waiting at the House of the Sun.

We immediately asked that she thank their majesties for this offer and said that we would be greatly honoured to attend.

The Maiden left to relay the message and soon returned asking us to join their royal majesties in the gallery. We were led there in order but were not kept waiting for long as the royal procession was ready to go but this time without music.

The Queen from yesterday went in front. She was wearing a small, expensive crown and dressed in white satin. She carried a small crucifix made from a pearl, which had been revealed by the young King and his Bride on this very day.

After the Queen, came the six maidens in two rows, carrying the King's items from the little altar. Next were three kings. The Bridegroom was in the middle of them. He wore plain, Italian-style clothing of black satin and a small black hat with a little pointed feather. He tipped his hat to us in greeting. We bowed to him and the others as we had been previously instructed.

After the kings came the three queens. Two were richly dressed but the one in the middle was, like the Bridegroom, all in black and Cupid was holding her train.

After they had passed, we were given the nod to follow. The maidens fell in behind us and Old Atlas took up the rear.

Our procession wound through many fine areas until we came to the

House of the Sun. We sat next to the King and Queen on a specially-built, richly decorated platform to watch the comedy.

We sat, spread about, on the right side of the kings with the maidens (except those who carried the Royal Standard and had their own place at the top), seated on the left side. All of the other attendants had to be content with standing between the columns to watch.

The comedy, as it turned out, had some quite extraordinary parts. I will briefly go over them:

ACT ONE

At the opening, a very old king came on together with his servants. A little chest that had been found floating on the water, was brought to his throne. Inside the chest was a delightful baby together with some jewels and small sealed parchment letter addressed to the King. The King opened it and read, bursting into tears as he did so. He told his servants that the King of the Moors had invaded his kinswoman's country, killing all the royalty except for this infant royal daughter who was intended to be betrothed to his son.

He swore revenge on the Moor and his allies and ordered that firstly, the child be lovingly looked after and secondly, to prepare for war against the Moor.

The upbringing and tutoring of the young lady took up most of the first act. She was assigned an elderly tutor once she grown up a little and with this and other situations, much entertainment ensued.

INTERVAL

In the interval a lion and a griffin were pitted against each other in a fight. The lion won and this was very entertaining.

ACT TWO

The second act introduced the Moor, a treacherous black man. He was furious when he found out that not only had his murders had been discovered but the little girl had escaped him too! He began working out how he would defeat the powerful enemy he had made and he was eventually given strategic advice by some refugees who had left their country because of famine and come to him.

Because of this and to our surprise, the young lady was recaptured. She would have been killed if it were not for his servants who fooled the Moor and disguised her. And so, the act closed with the spectacular triumph of the Moor.

ACT THREE

In the third act, a great army was raised against the Moor. It was put in the command of a brave, old knight. He led the army into the Moor's country and fought his way through until he finally rescued the young lady from the tower. She was restored to her royal robes.

After this, they built a glorious platform and placed the young lady on it. Twelve royal ambassadors came and the old knight gave a speech saying that the King had not only saved her life earlier but he had raised her as royalty (although she did not *always* behave in a manner befitting a young lady!).

He also declared that his royal majesty had originally chosen her to be wed to his son and wished that the wedding might finally go ahead, if they agreed to certain conditions. At this point, he read a long list of conditions from a scroll. All of them were quite good and proper. I would list them but it would take too long.

In short, the young lady swore to keep the conditions and in a dignified manner, expressed her gratitude for such a high honour.

The cast began to sing to the praise of God, the King and the young lady and left the stage.

INTERVAL

In the next interval we were shown the four beasts that Daniel saw in his vision[74]. They were described in great detail and each had its own unique significance.

ACT FOUR

The fourth act opened with the young lady returning to her lost kingdom and being crowned. She was led in a joyful procession around the court.

Ambassadors from all over the world presented themselves and wished her prosperity as well as admiring her in all her glory. However, this didn't last for long because she soon began to eye up the ambassadors and lords, flirting with them shamelessly. (The actress was a natural at doing this).

Before long, the Moor got to hear about her behaviour. He saw his chance and took the opportunity to sweet-talk her whilst her steward was not paying proper attention to her. She was easily swayed and did not stay faithful to the King, secretly entering into an affair with the Moor. The Moor seized his chance and continued to charm her until she even handed over control of her kingdom to him.

Then, in the third scene of this act, he turned on her and had her stripped naked and bound to a post on a wooden scaffold. She was whipped and then sentenced to death! This was so moving that many of us were crying at this point. Still naked, she was thrown into prison to await her death by poisoning. The poison failed to kill her but made her break out in sores all over.

For the most part, this was a sad and tragic act.

INTERVAL

For this interval, they brought in a likeness of Nebuchadnezzar, which had all kinds of heraldry on the head, chest, stomach, legs and feet. I will explain more later on.

ACT FIVE

In the fifth act, the young King was told of all that had gone on between the Moor and his future bride. He went to his father and begged that she was not left in that awful condition. His father agreed to help and sent ambassadors to do what they could for her sickness and captivity and also to rebuke her for her behaviour.

But she would not receive them and still agreed to be the Moor's mistress. The young King was informed of this.

INTERVAL

On this cliffhanger, a gang of fools came in carrying truncheons. In a flash, they built a globe of the world and then promptly unmade it again. It was an enjoyable bit of fantasy.

ACT SIX

Then it was time for the sixth act in which the young King went into battle against the Moor. Even though the Moor was beaten, everyone thought the King had also been killed in the battle. Eventually though, he returned, saved his intended and handed her to the safekeeping of his steward and chaplain. The steward was cruel to her and made her life a misery. Then it turned out that the priest was even more evil and managed to seize power for himself. The young King was told of what was happening and he sent one of his people who broke the priest's grip on power and saved the bride, who was then modestly dressed for her wedding.

INTERVAL

After the sixth act finished a huge artificial elephant was brought on.

He had a tower on his back, which held musicians. This proved very popular with the audience.

ACT SEVEN

It was time for the final act. The Bridegroom appeared in a spectacular ceremony. I had never seen anything like it and watched in amazement. The Bride joined him in a dignified and noble parade and the actors cried out 'LONG LIVE THE BRIDEGROOM! LONG LIVE THE BRIDE![75]'. In doing this, they were also giving their congratulations to the King and Queen in a fine manner. I could see that the royal couple were delighted by this.

The Bridegroom and Bride then paraded around the stage whilst the cast sang this song:

I
This lovely time
Brings so much joy
With the King's wedding.
So join us and sing
Loud and clear
That he who gave us all of this
Be forever happy.
II
The beautiful bride,
The one we have waited for

Shall be married to him.
And we have won
Following our struggles.
Believe in yourself
And be happy.

III
All our good seniors
After long service
Are now asked
To join in honour and multiply,
So thousands of descendants
Are of your bloodline.

After this song, thanks were returned and the comedy was happily concluded. The royals were especially delighted and, as the evening was drawing to a close, left in their procession.

We were expected to follow the royal parade up the winding stairs and into the hall. When we got there, we saw that the tables were already richly laid out and we were honoured to dine in the King's company for the first time.

The little altar was placed in the middle of the hall and the six royal banners were laid upon it.

The young King was the perfect host to us but seemed a little reserved and low. He chatted with us now and then but quite often sighed as if something was wrong. Each time he did, Cupid made fun of him and teased him.

The old King and Queen looked very solemn. In fact, only the wife of one of the older kings seemed at all cheerful but I could not work out why.

The royal family sat at the first table and we were all placed on the second. Some of the principal maidens sat at the third table and the rest of the maidens and men waited on the tables. This was done with great ceremony but it was very quiet and solemn. I'm afraid to comment on it too much but must give you at least some details:

Before the meal, all the royals had put on glittering snow-white clothes. Above their table hung the great gold crown. The precious stones in the crown shone so brightly that they could have lit the whole room on their own. All of the lights in the hall had been lit using the same small taper which was taken from the altar (I don't know the significance).

It fascinated me that the young King kept sending meat to the white serpent on the altar and I wondered why. Nearly all of the chatter at dinner came from little Cupid who would not leave us alone, especially me! Although he kept on and said all sorts of strange and funny things, no one was really laughing much. There was a strange atmosphere, almost as if something bad was about to happen. No music was played at any point and if anyone was asked anything, they just gave the briefest of replies and no one engaged in conversation. In short, the atmosphere was so strange and tense that sweat began to trickle down my body. Even the bravest man would have been unnerved by it.

With supper being nearly finished, the young King demanded that the book from the altar was brought over to him. He opened it and once again got an old man to read out an oath where we were asked to swear that we would stay faithful to the King, for better or worse. We all agreed, although with some trepidation. We were then asked if we were prepared to sign our names to that effect, which did not really give us much choice. So we went forward, one by one and each of us signed our names in the book.

When we had done this, the little crystal fountain was brought over. A small crystal glass was provided and all of the royals drank from the fountain. After they had finished, it was offered to us and then to everyone else present. This was called the 'Draught of Silence'[76].

Then, all the royals offered their hands and told us that, if we did not stand by them tonight, we would not see them again. This brought tears to our eyes. Our President spoke on our behalf and assured them of our support. They seemed content with this.

A little bell rang and all of the royals fell silent and looked so unbearably sad that we felt completely hopeless. They quickly removed their white robes and swapped them for black. The entire hall was then redecorated with black velvet, even the floor and ceiling (This had all been previously set up, ready to go).

The tables were removed and everyone sat around the platform. We were given black habits to wear.

Our President had gone out during this but she now returned holding six black taffeta scarves. She blindfolded the six royals using these.

Six covered coffins were brought in by the servants and put down in the hall. A low black seat was placed in the middle.

Finally, a tall, coal-black man entered. In his hand was a sharp axe. The old King was brought to the seat and, in an instant, his head was cut off! The head was wrapped in a black cloth and his blood was collected using a large gold goblet. This was placed into one of the coffins along with his body, covered and set aside.

And so it continued with each one of the royals. I thought I was next but it did not come to that for, as soon as the six had been beheaded, the black man went to leave. Another followed him and, just before he got to the door, his head was cut off too! They brought back his head together with his axe and placed them in a little chest.

I could not understand this all nor could I work out what was to come next at this Bloody Wedding. I just had to wait and see.

The Maiden could see that some of us were faltering. She tried to calm us and said 'Their lives are now in your hands. Follow me and their deaths shall mean life for many more'.

She told us not to trouble ourselves any further over it; to get a good night's sleep and everything would work out for them. She wished us goodnight and explained that she would keep watch over the bodies through the night.

This we did and our pages escorted us to our rooms. My page talked about various things (I still remember this well) and impressed me with his knowledge. I knew that he was only trying to calm me down so I could get some sleep but I could not get the image of the executions out of my mind. So I closed my eyes and pretended to sleep.

My room was overlooking the great lake and the windows were near to my bed so I could easily see it. I heard the clock strike midnight and shortly after, I saw what looked like a great fire on the lake. In fear, I opened the window and looked more closely. In the distance, I saw seven ships, full of lights, sailing towards us.

Above each of them, a flame hovered, It moved to and fro and sometimes dropped right down. I somehow knew that these were the spirits of the beheaded.

These ships gently approached the land and came to shore. I could see that there was only a single sailor on each. Then, our Maiden appeared carrying a torch and walked towards the ship. The six coffins followed behind her in a procession and each of them, together with the little chest were placed into the ships.

I awoke my page so he could see. He was very grateful as, having run up and down all day, he was so tired that he may have slept through it, even though he was expecting it.

As soon as the coffins were on board, all of the lights were put out and the six flames passed over the lake. Only a single light was left on each ship for the watchman.

There were also hundreds of watchmen who were camped on the shore and they now sent the Maiden back to the castle. She carefully bolted everything behind her so I could tell that nothing more was going to happen until daybreak.

So, we went back to bed. I was the only one of my company to have a room overlooking the lake and so the only one of us to witness it. I was extremely tired by this point and, even though my head was still spinning with thoughts, went to sleep.

CHAPTER FOUR: NOTES

[72] The inscription is in Latin and reads:

HERMES PRINCEPS.
POST TOT ILLATA GENERI HUMANO DAMNA,
DEI CONSILIO:
ARTISQUE ADMINICULO,
MEDICINA SALUBRIS FACTUS
HEIC FLUO.
Bibat ex me qui potest: lavet, qui vult: turbet qui audet:
BIBITE FRATRES, ET VIVITE

[73] This is often translated simply as 'arch' but the German reads 'Gewelbe' which is similar to the modern Gewölbe (vault) and is unlike 'Bogen', the usual word for an arch. However, Gewelbe was used in Middle-High German to describe an arch, vault or ceiling. I have used 'arched vault' as modern readers might visualize 'vault' as a crypt and 'arch' as a freestanding arch.

[74] Daniel 7:1-7

[1] In the first year of Belshazzar king of Babylon Daniel had a dream and visions of his head upon his bed: then he wrote the dream, and told the sum of the matters.
[2] Daniel spake and said, I saw in my vision by night, and, behold, the four winds of the heaven strove upon the great sea.
[3] And four great beasts came up from the sea, diverse one from another.
[4] The first was like a lion, and had eagle's wings: I beheld till the wings thereof were plucked, and it was lifted up from the earth, and made stand upon the feet as a man, and a man's heart was given to it.
[5] And behold another beast, a second, like to a bear, and it raised up itself on one side, and it had three ribs in the mouth of it between the teeth of it: and they said thus unto it, Arise, devour much flesh.
[6] After this I beheld, and lo another, like a leopard, which had upon the back of it four wings of a fowl; the beast had also four heads; and dominion was given to it.
[7] After this I saw in the night visions, and behold a fourth beast, dreadful and terrible, and strong exceedingly; and it had great iron teeth: it devoured and brake in pieces, and stamped the residue with the feet of it: and it was diverse from all the beasts that were before it; and it had ten horns.

[75] 'vivat Sponsus: vivat Sponsa'

[76] Haustus Silentii

CHAPTER FIVE

Chapter Five
The Fifth Day

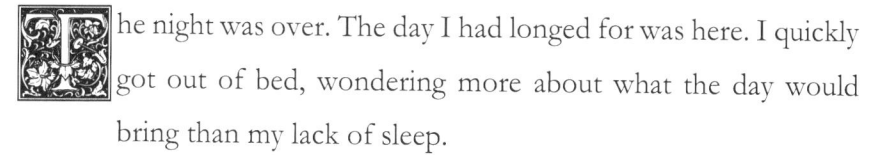

The night was over. The day I had longed for was here. I quickly got out of bed, wondering more about what the day would bring than my lack of sleep.

After I had dressed and gone downstairs, it was still early and there was no one else in the hall. I asked my page to take me around the castle and show me something interesting.

He was keen as ever and took me down some steps and beneath the ground. We arrived at a great iron door with writing in copper letters upon it[77]:

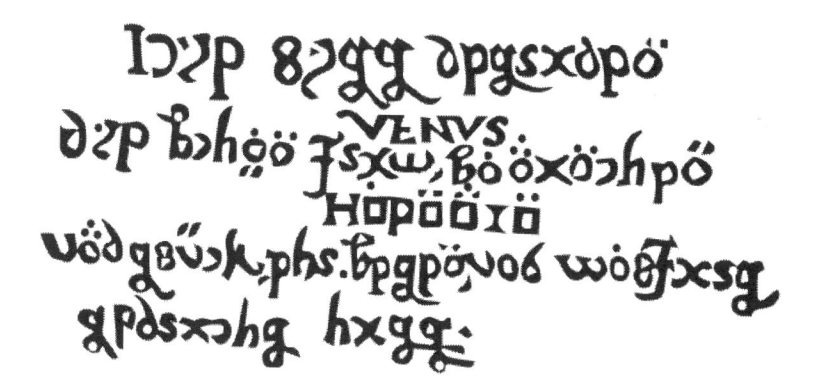

'Here lies buried *Venus, the beautiful woman who has brought luck, honour, blessings and prosperity to many a great man*'.

I copied this into my notebook.

The page opened the door and, taking my hand, led me through a dark passage until we came to a very small door, which was unlocked. My page informed me that it had been opened yesterday to take out the coffins and had not been locked again since then.

As soon as we entered, I saw the most precious creation of nature. The vault was lit only by enormous red jewels[78]. The page told me that we were inside the King's Treasury.

But the outstanding thing in this room was a magnificent tomb, so richly ornate that I wondered aloud why it was not guarded. 'You can thank your lucky stars,' said the page 'you are seeing something that no other person, outside the royal family, has ever seen'.

The tomb was triangular and a large, polished copper bowl was set into the middle. The rest of it was pure gold and precious stones. In the bowl stood the figure of an angel. The angel was holding a tree that I did not recognise. Fruit dropped continuously from the tree and into the bowl. As soon as each fruit touched the water, it turned into water itself. As the water overflowed, it ran into three small golden bowls nearby. This little altar was supported by three animals; an eagle, an ox and a lion[79], which stood on an exquisitely-made base.

'What does it mean?' I asked the page

He repeated the inscription on the door:

Here lies buried Venus, the beautiful woman who has brought luck, honour, blessings and prosperity to many a great man'.

He then pointed out a trapdoor made of copper.

'If you like, we can go further down'

'Lead on' I replied

I went down the steps and into the pitch black. The page immediately opened a little chest, which contained an ever-burning candle. He lit a nearby torch with this. I grew quite frightened and concerned and asked him whether we were supposed to be here.

'A long as the royal family sleep, there is nothing to fear' he answered.

Then I saw an ornate bed, with unusual curtains all around it. The page drew one aside and I gasped to see the Lady Venus lying there. The page pulled off the sheets and she was stark naked before me and so beautiful that I was almost beside myself with surprise. She lay there, unmoving. I could not tell if she was a statue or an actual human corpse lying there, dead. I did not dare to touch her.

The page covered her up again and drew the curtains. I did not see her move.

Behind the bed, on a plaque, was written[80]:

CHAPTER FIVE

I asked my page about the inscription. He laughed and told me that I would find out soon enough.

He extinguished the torch as we climbed out. As we left, I looked more closely at the little doors and noticed that at each corner burned a small taper of pyrites. I hadn't noticed this before, as the fire was so clear that it looked more like a jewel than a taper. The heat was continually melting the tree, although it kept on producing fruit.

'Now listen.' said the page 'this is what I heard Atlas telling the King:

'When the fruits of my tree have completely melted, I will awake and be mother of a king.'

Whilst he was saying this, little Cupid flew in. At first, he was quite embarrassed to see us but when he saw us looking so shocked, as if we had seen a ghost, he burst out laughing.

'What ghost brought you two here?' he asked.

I stammered out that I had been lost whilst wandering in the castle and just happened to wander in here by mistake. I added that the page had been looking for me and found me in here. I hoped that I hadn't done anything wrong.

'Well, that's fair enough then, my nosy old father' said Cupid 'but I wouldn't have been best pleased if you had noticed this door. I had best sort it now!'

He put a strong padlock on the copper trapdoor and secured it. I was thanking God that he had not come in earlier. My page was relieved that I had covered for him so well.

'Although…' Cupid mused, 'you came very close to stumbling in on my dear mother and I can't let that go'.

He put the point of his arrow into one of the little tapers to heat it and then stabbed it on my hand! I paid little attention to it at the time; I was just glad that we had got off so lightly.

By the time we returned to the hall, my companions were up. I joined them as if I had just woken. Cupid came in after he had finished securing everything downstairs and asked me to show him my hand. I did and he laughed, as there was still a drop of blood on my hand. He told the others to look after me, as I wouldn't last long!

We all wondered how Cupid could be so cheery, given the grim events of yesterday, but it did not seem to have bothered him in the slightest.

Our President had prepared herself to travel and was all in black velvet, still carrying her customary laurel branch. Her maidens carried their branches too. Everything was ready so the Maiden told us to have something to drink and prepare for the procession. We did not hang about and followed her out of the hall and into the courtyard.

There stood six coffins. My companions assumed that the six royals were inside but, of course, I knew better.

However, I did not know what was going on with these coffins. Next to each coffin were eight masked men. Mournful music began to play and I was stunned by the deep sadness of the melody. The men lifted the coffins and we began a procession, following them into the garden, which had a wooden structure in the centre. On its roof was a glorious crown supported by seven columns. It was separated into six graves inside with a stone by each and a rounded, hollow stone standing up in the middle.

The coffins were solemnly lowered into the graves and the stones were used to seal them. The little chest was placed in the middle. My companions were fooled by all of this, thinking that the bodies were inside. On top of it all was a great flag painted with a phoenix, probably to reinforce the illusion. I thanked God that I had seen and knew more than the others did.

After the burials, the Maiden sat on the stone in the middle and gave a short speech about how we should not shirk from our tasks and not to fret over the pains we would have to endure but to take part in returning the royals to life again. She asked us to rise and come with her to the Tower of Olympus where we could collect medicines, which would enable us to do this.

We agreed to this and followed her through another little door, which led to the shore. There stood the seven ships, now empty. The maidens placed their laurel branches by each and split us between the six ships. They sent us off on our journey in the name of God and stood on the shore, watching us until we were out of sight. They returned to the castle with the watchmen.

Each of our ships had a unique flag. Five of them depicted the five Platonic solids[81] whilst mine, which also carried the Maiden, bore a globe. Each ship was manned by two sailors and we sailed in a special order. The lead ship had twelve musicians and I thought that the Moor was also carried aboard. This ship's flag was the pyramid.

The 'Pyramid' ship sailed at the front with Ships B, C and D, as I will call them, in a line behind. I sat in ship C.

Behind us came the most impressive of the ships, which I'll call E and F. They had many laurel branches on board but no passengers. They also had Sun and Moon flags.

Bringing up the rear was a single ship (G) which carried forty maidens.

We sailed over the lake in this order and then through a narrow channel and into the open sea. Sirens, nymphs and sea-goddesses were waiting there for us and a mermaid swam over to us with a gift given in honour of the wedding.

This gift was a huge pearl, a perfect sphere and set beautifully. The likes of it had never been seen in the Old World or even our Modern World. Our Maiden received it with grateful thanks. The nymph then asked if we would drop anchor for a little while so they could entertain us.

The Maiden was happy to do this and commanded the ships to halt with the two great ships in the middle, whilst the rest surrounded them in a pentagon shape.

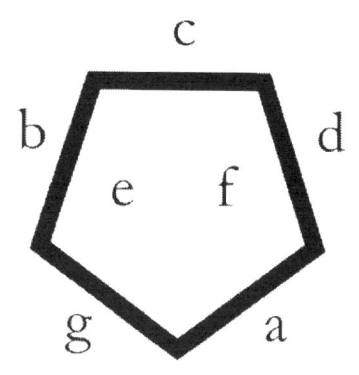

The nymphs formed a circle around the ships and began to sing with the most delicate and sweet voices:

I
There is nothing better on Earth
Than lovely, honourable love.
It brings us to God
And we love our neighbours.
So sing this to the King
So it's heard throughout the seas.
We ask and you answer.

II
What has brought us to life?
It's love.
Who has brought back grace?

It's love.

How are we born?

From love.

How is all lost?

Without love.

III

Who brought us into the world?

It was Love.

Why were we raised?

For Love.

What do we owe our parents?

It's Love.

Why are they so patient?

From Love.

IV

What overcomes all things?

It's Love.

How do we find love?

Through Love.

Where do you see a man's good work?

In Love.

Who can bring two together?

It's Love.

V
So let us sing
Loud and clear
To honour love
So there is more.
With our Lord King and Queen
Their bodies here, their souls have gone.

VI
And as we live
So shall God give.
Where love and grace
Did tear them apart
The flame of love
Will make them one.

VII
This song will come
With greatest joy
Through a thousand generations
And into eternity.

They finished the song with a flourish and the loveliest melody. I saw now why Ulysses had plugged the ears of his men because I felt like the saddest man in the world. Sad because nature had not made me as beautiful as these creatures.

Our Maiden soon sent them away so we could sail once more. She presented the nymphs with a long red scarf as a token of appreciation and they swam away happily.

It was right about now that I started to feel the effects of Cupid's arrow. I do not see that going into detail is going to be of any benefit to the reader so I will say no more. But this was the wound that I was warned about in my dream at the beginning. So, take warning from my example – if you hang around Venus' bed, Cupid will be after you!

A few hours passed and we spent our time engaging in friendly chat. We soon saw the Tower of Olympus and the Maiden commanded that signals be fired to announce our arrival.

A great white flag was unfurled in response and a small, golden sailboat came out to meet us. On board was a very old man, the Warder of the Tower, and guards who were dressed in white. We were greeted in a friendly manner and escorted to the tower.

The tower stood on an island, which was a perfect square. The outer wall was so thick that I counted two hundred and sixty steps to pass through it.

On the other side of the wall was a lovely meadow dotted about with small gardens. There were fruits that I did not recognise growing in the gardens.

There was an inner wall too and the tower looked more like seven round towers built one inside another, with the tallest in the middle. Inside, they all connected and were seven stories high.

We entered the gate and were ushered to one side against the wall. I could see that this was so they could get the coffins into the tower without us seeing, but the others did not suspect a thing.

They must have finished doing this, as then we were taken to the bottom of the tower. It was nicely decorated but there was no time to relax because this was actually a laboratory. We had to crush and wash plants, precious stones and all sorts of things, extracting juice and essences and collecting them in glassware, which we handed over.

Our Maiden was very organised and detailed everything that we needed to do. She assigned tasks efficiently to each of us, to the extent that we were merely drones carrying out the work as per her instructions until we had prepared everything that was necessary to revive the beheaded corpses.

In the meantime (as was later explained to me), three maidens were in the first room carefully washing the bodies.

When we had almost finished our work, some broth and a small glass of wine was brought in for refreshment. It was hardly a feast but we were clearly not here for leisure. Even when we had finished the day's work, we had to make do with mattresses placed on the ground to sleep on.

I was not too bothered about sleeping though, so went for a walk around the garden. I walked as far as the wall and because the night sky was very clear, I spent some time observing the stars as I walked.

By chance, I came across steps leading to the top of the wall. As the moon was bright, I could see well enough to be confident about climbing the steps and went up to the top. I looked out over the sea, which was dead calm.

Having such a good opportunity to survey the stars, I soon realised that a rare conjunction of planets could be observed. I was looking over the sea as midnight struck and, off in the distance, I saw the seven flames moving over the sea towards me. They moved onwards and eventually went to the top of the spire on the tower.

It became quite frightening because, as soon as the flames had settled, the wind began to blow strongly and the waves on the sea started to become rough. The moon clouded over and my terror built as I hurried down the steps whilst I could still see. I barely made it to the bottom in time and hurried straight indoors. Whether the flames stayed where they were or flew off again, I have no idea. I did not dare to go outside in the darkness and storm again.

And so, I went to my mattress and lay down there. The gentle sounds of a murmuring fountain in the laboratory soon lulled me off to sleep and so ended the fifth day with more exciting adventures.

CHAPTER FIVE: NOTES

[77] The writing on the copper plate uses symbols in place of letters to record the (approximate) phrase '*Hier ligg begraben Venus die schön Frau, so manchen hohen Mann um Glück, Ehre, Segen und Wohlfahrt gebracht hatt*'. Here lies buried Venus, the beautiful woman who has brought luck, honour, blessings and prosperity to many a great man.

[78] The jewels are described as 'carbuncles' which is a term most commonly used to describe red gemstones (usually red garnets). There is a Sherlock Holmes story 'The Adventure of the Blue Carbuncle', the titular stone's rarity in this tale being due to its unusual colour; Holmes remarking at one point that it bears every characteristic of a carbuncle save that is not ruby red.

[79] The book of Ezekiel describes the chariot of God which is borne by cherubim described thus: '*As for the likeness of their faces, they four had the face of a man, and the face of a lion, on the right side: and they four had the face of an ox on the left side; they four also had the face of an eagle*'. Ezekiel 1:10

[80] Another symbol/letter substitution code which is (approximately) '*Wenn die Frucht meines Baum wird vollends verschmelzen, werde ich aufwachen und eine Mutter sein eines Königs*'. When the fruits of my tree have completely melted, I will awake and be mother of a king.

[81] *Corpora Regularia* – the regular geometrical three-dimensional bodies described in Plato's 'Timaeus'. Plato hypothesized that the classical elements were made of these shapes:

NAME	FACES	ELEMENT
Tetrahedron	Four	Fire
Cube	Six	Earth
Octahedron	Eight	Air
Dodecahedron	Twelve	Aether
Icosahedron	Twenty	Water

CHAPTER SIX

Chapter Six

The Sixth Day

The next morning after we had all woken up, we sat and chatted about what we thought might happen next. Some of us thought that they would all be brought back to life. Others disagreed because they thought that the deaths of the oldest would restore and give extra life to the younger ones. Some reckoned that they hadn't really been killed but others had been substituted and beheaded instead.

We talked about this for quite a while until the old man came in and said good morning. He looked around to see if everything was ready. We had done our jobs to the letter and he could not fault anything so he took all of the glasses we had prepared and placed them into a case.

Soon after, some young men entered. They brought in ladders, ropes and large wings, which they put on the floor in front of us. The old man addressed us:

'My dear sons, each one of you needs to carry three things for the whole day. You can choose which you want to take or draw lots if you prefer; it's up to you'.

'We'll choose' we replied in unison.

'No,' he said 'draw lots instead'.

So he wrote out three notes. On one, he wrote 'Ladder', then 'Rope' and 'Wings' on the other two. He put them into a hat and we each had to draw our lot. Those who drew the ropes thought they had got the best one. I ended up with a ladder, which was quite a struggle for me. It was twelve feet long and heavy and I had to carry it whilst those with ropes could just coil them around their bodies. As for the wings, the old man tied them so well onto everyone in the third group, it was as if they had grown them!

He turned the tap to shut off the fountain and we had to remove it from the centre of the room and out of the way. After everything was cleared, he left, taking the case of glasses with him. He locked the door after himself, so we were pretty much trapped in the tower.

But, only quarter of an hour later, a round hole at the top of the tower was opened and our Maiden was there, looking down at us. She called out 'Good morning!' to us and told us to come up. Those who had the wings immediately shot up into the air and straight through the hole. We climbed our ladders but were told to pull them straight up when we got to the top. Only those who had the ropes were in trouble. Finally, they got the ropes onto an iron hook and each man had to physically climb up the rope as best as he could manage. This was not accomplished without blisters!

As soon as we were all up, the hole was covered again and the Maiden turned to us and greeted us all in a friendly way. The room we were in was the whole width of the tower and had six very grand vestries, which were raised above the floor with three steps leading up to each.

We were placed in the vestries and instructed to pray for the life of the King and Queen. The Maiden left us to it and went out through a small door.

As soon as we had finished our prayers, the small door opened again and twelve people entered. I recognised them as the musicians from yesterday. They brought in a strange object, a sort of long shape which my companions thought was a fountain. They placed it in the middle of the room. I worked out that the corpses must be inside; its oval inner shape was easily big enough to hold them all if they were placed close together.

The twelve of them left and fetched their instruments so they could accompany the Maiden and her female attendants. They played light and delicate music as the Maiden carried her casket. The others held branches and small lamps and a few had lighted torches. The torches were handed straight to us and we were told to stand around the fountain in this order:

$$\begin{array}{c} ooooooooo\,a \\ o OOOO o \\ OOOOOOOOO \\ c\ {}^{oooo}_{oooo} O\ {}^{oooo}_{oooo}\ b \\ oooo A ooo \\ oOOOOo \\ ooooooooo\,d \end{array}$$

First was the Maiden (A) with her attendants circling her and holding the lamps and branches (c). We were next and stood with our torches (b). Next were the musicians in single file (a). Finally, the rest of the maidens who were also in single file (d).

I do not know where the other maidens came from. They may have lived in the castle or been brought in overnight. All of their faces were veiled in a delicate white linen so I could not recognise any of them.

Now, the Maiden opened her casket and took out something round, which was double-wrapped in green taffeta. She put this on the uppermost container and covered it with a lid, which had holes made in it. She poured some of the liquid we had made the day before onto the rim of the lid. The spring immediately started flowing and ran through four small pipes and into the container. Underneath the lower container were a number of points where the maidens placed their lamps to heat the container. The liquid began to boil and dripped through many small holes and onto the bodies beneath, dissolving them all and turning them into a liquor.

Although my companions did not know it, I calculated that the wrapped-up object was the Moor's head, which heated the liquid so fiercely.

There were many holes around the big container and the maidens stuck their branches into them. Whether it was a vital part of the process or whether it was simply a part of the ceremony, I do not know. The branches were continually splashed by the spring and an even deeper yellow liquid dripped from them and dropped into the container. This lasted for nearly two hours with the spring constantly running by itself. Eventually, it began to slow and trickle.

During this, the musicians departed leaving us to wander about the room. There was certainly plenty to see; there were pictures, paintings, clockwork mechanisms, organs, fountains and much, much more of interest.

When the spring had slowed down to a slight trickle, the Maiden called for a golden globe to be brought over. She turned a tap at the bottom of the spring and allowed the liquid matter, which had been dissolved by the hot liquid, to pour into the globe. Some of it flowed out as a very red liquid. The rest of the liquid, which remained in the top vessel was poured away, making the spring much lighter. The spring was then taken away. I do not know whether it was opened up elsewhere or even if anything useful remained of the bodies that were inside.

What I do know is that the liquid that was emptied into the globe was heavier than six or more of us could manage. Looking at it though, you would have expected one man to be able to carry it.

However, after a bit of a struggle, it was carried out and we were left alone once more. I could hear footsteps above us and kept one eye on my ladder.

My companions had all sorts of strange theories about the spring. They, of course, thought that the bodies lay in the castle garden so could not make the connection. I thanked God that I had woken up when I had and witnessed what I did. It had helped me all the more in understanding the work of our Maiden.

After a quarter of an hour, the trapdoor in the ceiling opened again and we were commanded to come up. As before, the wings, ladders and ropes were used to do so. It annoyed me that the maidens could get upstairs by another way but we were left to struggle. I guessed that there must be some reason for it, other than to give the old man something to do in handing out the ladders, ropes and wings. Even those who had been given the wings gained no advantage other than now when we had to climb through the hole in the ceiling. Having got up there again and the trapdoor closed behind us, I saw the globe which was now hanging by a strong chain in the centre of the room. There was nothing else in the room other than windows and, between every pair of windows, a door, which covered a large polished mirror. The windows and mirrors were positioned so that when the sun (which was shining very brightly at this time) shone on one of the doors there appeared to be suns all around the room. The reflections were concentrated on the polished golden globe in the middle and it was so bright we could not look at it but instead were forced to look out of the windows whilst the globe was heated up to the required temperature.

I can honestly say that it was the most wonderful spectacle of nature. There appeared to be suns everywhere and the globe in the middle shone even brighter until, just like the sun itself, we could not look at it for any longer than a glance.

Finally, the Maiden ordered the doors to be closed on the mirrors and the windows closed again to let the globe cool down a little. It was about seven o'clock at this point. We were quite pleased as we thought that we would now have time for some breakfast. However, we need not have worried about overindulging, as the main nourishment we were offered was philosophical! None of us minded though. The Maiden made us so happy with her assurances of good things in the future that we forgot any troubles we had.

And I can speak for my esteemed companions too when I say that our minds were never on food. Our only wish was to take part in this scientific adventure and, in doing so, think about the Creator's power and wisdom.

After we had our meal, we settled down to work. The globe had cooled and we had to physically lift it off the chain and place it upon the floor. We were told that it would need to be divided into two along the middle. There followed a discussion over the best way to achieve this. We concluded that a sharp pointed diamond would do the job.

We opened the globe in this way. Inside there was no trace of redness any more, just a large and beautiful snow-white egg. We were delighted that it had turned out so well, as the Maiden had been concerned that the shell may not have been strong enough. We stood around and looked at it, each one of us as proud and happy as if we had laid it ourselves! However, the Maiden soon ordered it to be taken away and left with it. As always, she locked the door behind her.

Whether she (or anyone else) did something else with it outside, I do not know for sure but I do not think so.

We had to wait another quarter of an hour until a third hole was opened. We had to clamber up using our tools as before until we got to the fourth floor.

In this room, we found a huge copper vessel filled with yellow sand and warmed by a gentle fire. The egg was placed in it and the sand raked over to incubate it.

The copper vessel was square and had these two verses written in large letters on one side:

O. BLI. TO. BIT. MI. LI.

KANT. I. VOLT. BIT. TO. GOLT

On the second side were these three words:

SANITAS. NIX. HASTA.[82]

The third had only one word:

F.I.A.T.[83]

But on the last was a complete inscription[84], which read:

What

Fire: Air: Water: Earth:

Could not extract from the holy ashes of our kings and queens was gathered in this urn by the faithful band of alchemists. A.D.

Now, whether this referred to the egg or sand, I will leave for scholars to argue. I am just recording the facts.

Our egg was now ready and was removed. It did not need us to crack it because the bird within soon broke out. He appeared very happy to be out although he was very bloody and misshapen. We placed him on the warm sand. The Maiden told us to tie him securely or he would be no end of trouble when we fed him.

We did this and then food was brought in. This appeared to be the blood of the beheaded, diluted with the liquid we had prepared. As soon as he had some of this, the bird grew quickly before our very eyes and we could soon see why the Maiden had warned us to tie him securely! He pecked and scratched with such force that if he had gotten free he would surely have killed one of us!

He was wild and completely black, so he was given different food, possibly the blood of one of the other royals. After he had eaten this, all of his black feathers moulted and snow-white feathers grew in their place. He became much more docile but none of us quite trusted him yet!

After a third feeding his feathers began to colour. In all my life, I have never seen such beautiful colours! At the same time, he became incredibly tame and friendly, so much so that the Maiden allowed us to untie him.

She said 'Thanks to all your hard work and the permission of our old man, this bird has been brought to life and achieved perfection. I'd say that this is a good reason for us to celebrate!'

She then ordered our lunch to be brought in. She told us that the hardest part of the work was now over and we should relax and enjoy ourselves. And so, we began to celebrate but we were still wearing our mourning clothes which dampened the mood a little.

The Maiden was continually curious about us. Possibly this was to find out which of us might be useful to her in future work. Tonight she talked mostly about smelting[85] and was very pleased when one of us turned out to be something of an expert in the field and was well-acquainted with the many books on the subject.

The lunch only lasted three quarters of an hour and most of the time was spent feeding the bird. We needed to constantly feed him but he had stopped growing at this point. After dinner, we were not given much time to digest our food before the Maiden left with the bird.

The fifth room was opened and we entered as before and offered our services. We had to prepare a bath for the bird. The water was coloured with a fine white powder, which gave it the appearance of milk. It started off cool and we placed the bird into it. He was very happy with this, drinking the water and playing about in it. Soon after though, it began to warm up due to the lamps that were placed underneath and it was all we could do to keep him in the bath. We placed a cover over the bath and he poked his head out through a hole in the top. The heat increased and he began to lose his feathers in the bath until he was as smooth as a baby. I was astonished that the heat did him no harm other than losing the feathers, which had dissolved in the bath, turning the water blue.

Finally, we took off the cover and he hopped out of the bath. He was shiny and smooth, which was a lovely sight. However, he was still somewhat wild so we fitted him with a collar and chain and walked him up and down the room.

Meanwhile, the fire was stoked up under the bath and the water boiled away leaving a blue stone, which we removed. We crushed the stone and ground it up. We used this to paint the bird's skin. He looked very strange when we had finished as the head was left white whilst the rest of him was blue.

With this, our work at this level was done and (after the Maiden and blue bird had left us) we were called up to the sixth floor where things started to get disturbing.

In the middle of the room was a small altar, which was similar to the one in the King's Hall. The same six objects were upon it with the bird making a seventh. The little fountain was placed in front of the bird and he drank from it. Then he pecked the white snake until it bled quite badly. We were told to collect the blood in a golden cup and make the bird drink it. The bird struggled and we had to force it to drink by pouring it down his throat. We dipped the snake's head in the fountain and the snake revived, slithered back into the death's head and stayed out of sight.

Meanwhile, the sphere was revolving until it hit a particular conjunction. Immediately, the watch struck one, which set off another conjunction. The watch then struck two and another conjunction started to align. We watched the third conjunction and watch striking when the bird laid its neck down on the book and allowed its head to be chopped off by one of us, who was chosen by chance. Not a drop of blood flowed from the beheading but, when his breast was cut open, blood as fresh and clear as a fountain of rubies spurted out.

We felt his death deeply but we knew that a mere bird was of little use and so we put it out of our minds and continued.

The altar was moved aside and we helped the Maiden to burn the body to ashes together with a small plaque that was nearby. The fire was kindled with the little candle, which we also used to purify the ashes before placing them in a box made of cypress wood.

I must now tell you about the trick that was played on three others and me:

After we had collected the ashes, the Maiden began to speak:

'My lords, we are now in the sixth room and have only one more to go. Then all our troubles will come to an end and we will return to the castle and wake up our most gracious lords and ladies.

I would like to commend you all to our King and Queen so you can all receive a suitable reward. That is, I *would* like to but can't...'

She pointed at me and three others, as she continued

'...because these four slackers really don't deserve it!

Because I am very fond of you all, I am not going to turn them in to get the punishment they deserve but I cannot let it lie. So, I have decided to exclude them from the seventh and final floor, which is the best and ultimate level. This way, they can't mess it up for the rest of you and you won't get blamed by their royal majesties'.

You can imagine what a state we were in when we heard this. The Maiden kept such a straight face that we were in tears and felt that we were the unhappiest men in the world. The Maiden got one of the many maids to fetch the musicians, who escorted us from the room, blowing their cornets with such derision and scorn that they could hardly play for laughing at us. It was even more upsetting that the Maiden was enjoying our distress and humiliation so much. Even some of our companions didn't look bothered by all of this, which made it worse.

But – it all changed once we were outside the door. The musicians turned around and told us to cheer up and follow them up the winding staircase. They led us right up to a point above the seventh floor, directly under the roof. The old man, who we had not seen up until this point, was standing next to a little round furnace. He welcomed us in the friendliest way and congratulated us, explaining that the Maiden had chosen us especially for this!

We explained to him what had happened and how frightened and upset we had been. When he heard this, he almost split his sides laughing and could barely speak to us for his laughter.

'Well, my dear boys,' he said 'it just goes to show that you never know what God has got planned for you!'

As he was speaking, the Maiden came in carrying her little box. She took one look at us and burst out laughing!

After she had composed herself, she emptied the ashes into another container and filled the box with other stuff, explaining that she now had to see the others and pull the wool over *their* eyes. She told us that, in the meantime, we must obey the old man's instructions and work as well and hard as we had before.

With this, she left us and went into the seventh room. We heard her call our companions but what happened next, I have no idea; we were too busy working to look down through the ceiling at them and, when I asked some of them later, found that they were forbidden to discuss it.

But this was what we did: we took the previously prepared liquid and had to dampen the ashes until they bound together like a thin dough. We heated this over the fire then, still hot, we poured it into two little moulds and left it to cool a little.

As we were waiting, we had a quick look at our companions below. They were all stood around a furnace and using pipes to blow the flames higher. Each one of them was frantically blowing the fire as if they were the 'chosen ones' and oh-so-important. They kept on until the old man called us back to work and we had to stop watching them. I do not know what they were up to after this.

We opened up our little moulds and revealed two beautiful, bright and translucent figures, the likes of which had never been seen by human eyes before now. There was a male and a female, both about four inches long. What was most surprising was that they were not hard and solid but supple and fleshy, like a real human body. But they were not alive and I was reminded of the figure of Lady Venus that the page had shown me; she was probably made in the same way.

We placed this angelic little pair on two satin cushions and just looked at them for a long time, admiring the exquisite beauty of their forms.

The old lord told us to come away and get back to work. We had to take the golden cup containing the bird's blood and drip it continually into the mouths of the little figures so they would grow. If they were beautiful when they were small, they became proportionally more so as they increased in size. Every artist should have been present to see this so they would see how nature could put their skills to shame.

They grew so large that we removed them from the little cushions and moved them to a long table, covered in white velvet.

The old man also instructed us to cover them up to the breast with a piece of fine white double taffeta, although it was a real shame to cover up such beauty.

They grew to their perfect size before we had used up all of the blood. They had golden-yellow curly hair and even the figure of Venus paled by comparison.

But there was no warmth or responsiveness in them. They were dead figures even though they looked alive. We had to be careful that they did not grow any more so the old man told us to stop the feeding and cover their faces with the silk. Next, torches were placed all around the table. You may think that the torches were a necessary part of this but they were not. The old man only wanted them present so we would not see when the soul entered them. However, I had seen these flames twice before so knew what I was looking for. (I did not mention this to the old man or my companions though).

He asked us to sit on a bench by the table. Soon after, the Maiden entered with the usual musical accompaniment and attendants. She carried two strange white garments unlike anything that I had seen in the castle. I am hard-put to describe them; they looked like crystal but they were soft and translucent.

She laid them down on a table and got her maidens to sit there on a bench. She and the old man began all manner of magical-looking motions but it was clearly designed to misdirect us.

As I said before, this was all done directly below the roof, which was an impressive construction. On the inside it arched upwards, divided into seven hemispheres the central one being the highest. At the top was a little round hole, which was closed. Nobody else noticed this hole.

After much ceremony, six maidens entered, each carrying a large trumpet, which had a glittering, glowing green material wrapped around it like a wreath. The old man took one of these and went to the top of the table. He removed some of the torches and stood over the bodies, removing the covers from their faces. Placing the trumpet in the mouth of one, he positioned it so it was pointed towards the little hole in the roof.

My companions focused on the bodies at this point but I had other ideas and looked at the roof. As soon as the foliage wrapped around the trumpet was lit on fire, I saw the hole at the top open and a stream of fire passed through the hole, down the trumpet and shot into the body. The hole was covered again and the trumpet was removed.

The misdirection worked on my companions; they imagined that the setting on fire of the foliage had given life to the figure. For, as soon as the soul entered the body, the eyes twinkled with life although there was little movement.

He repeated the actions of placing the trumpet in the mouth and lighting the material, doing this three times for each figure. Then all of the lights were put out and taken away. The velvet coverings were lifted and thrown over the bodies. A birthing bed was then unlocked and they were carried over to it. The covers were taken off them and they were laid side by side. The curtains were drawn and they slept for a good while.

It was now time for the Maiden to go and check on the other workers. She told me later on that they were all really pleased because they got to make gold. This is certainly part of our art but it is certainly not the best, nor the most important or essential part of it.

Like us, they had been given some of the ashes but they imagined that the bird was provided only to produce gold and that, somehow, this would restore life to the dead.

Meanwhile, we sat very still, waiting for the spouses to awake. We were there for half an hour until Cupid appeared again and after greeting us all, flew behind the curtain where he tormented the poor couple until they woke up!
They were astonished by this, as they thought that they had simply been asleep since losing their heads. Cupid reintroduced them to each other and backed off to give them a little time to get orientated.

Of course, this meant he was back to playing his tricks on us instead! At one point he wanted the musicians to play and make the place livelier.

Soon after, the Maiden returned and humbly greeted the King and Queen (they were still rather groggy at this stage). She kissed their hands and presented them with the two beautiful garments we saw earlier, which they put on.
There were two beautiful chairs prepared for them and they sat in these. We congratulated them respectfully and the King thanked us and wished us well.

It was already around five o'clock, so they could not stay any longer. As soon as all their important items were loaded, we accompanied them down the stairs, through the doors and outside to the ship. They got on board and departed with some of the maidens and Cupid. The ship sailed off at speed and we soon lost sight of it. I was later told that they were met and escorted by other majestic ships. So, in four hours' time, they were many leagues out at sea.

After five o'clock, the musicians were told to carry all of our things back to the ships in preparation for the return journey. This was taking rather a long time so the old lord ordered a party of his concealed soldiers to show themselves and assist. They had been hidden along the walls and we had not noticed them at all. I could now see that the tower was well protected against attack.

The soldiers made quick work of the loading and nothing now remained but to go to supper.

The table was already set out and the Maiden accompanied us back to our companions. She told us not to let on what we had been doing but to pretend that we were still sad because we had been kicked out – no laughing!

Most of our companions exchanged smug looks and smiled at one another although some of them sympathised with us.

The old lord joined us at supper and directed our conversations. Whatever anyone spoke of he was able to disprove it, correct it or volunteer further information on the subject. I learned a great deal from him. It would be good if everyone could learn from him and follow his methods, for then there would not be so many things wrong in the world.

After we had finished our evening meal, the old lord showed us his cabinets of curiosities[86], which were dotted here and there along the walls. We saw such marvels of nature and creations of man's invention that we would need an entire year to properly examine them. And so, we viewed them by candlelight long into the night until we needed sleep more than we needed to see any more rarities.

We were put up in rooms in the wall. The bedrooms were finely decorated and had very expensive and good quality beds. It made us wonder why we had been given such rough accommodation the day before.

With all the hard work done and nothing more to worry about, the gentle sounds of the sea soon lulled me into a deep sleep. I dreamt and slept soundly from eleven o'clock until eight the next morning.

CHAPTER SIX: NOTES

[82] SANITAS. NIX. HASTA. (Health, Snow, Spear)

[83] Let it be done

[84]   *QUOD.*
Ignis: Aer: Aqua: Terra:
SANCTIS REGUM ET REGINARUM NOSTR:
Cineribus.
Eripere non potuerunt
Fidelis Chymicorum Turba
IN HANC URNAM
Contulit.

                              Ad

[85] The word here is *schmelzen* (to melt or liquefy). I have taken this to refer specifically to the process of extracting metals from ore and the English 'smelting' is probably the most accurate translation.

[86] The *Kunstkammer* or *Wunderkabinett* (Cabinet of wonders) were collections of objects that were precursors to our modern museums. Unlike museums, the collections were not categorised and mixed natural objects with art, historic and modern artefacts (sometimes produced specifically for the collection).

CHAPTER SEVEN

Chapter Seven

The Seventh Day

I woke up after eight o'clock and quickly got dressed, ready to return to the tower. However, the dark passages in the wall were like a maze and I wandered for quite a while before I could find my way out.

The others were in the same boat too but we all finally gathered at the lowest vault. We were given all-yellow clothes and our Golden Fleeces. The Maiden informed us that we were Knights of the Golden Stone (which we had not realized before now).

After we dressed in these clothes and ate our breakfast, the old man came round and gave each one of us a gold medal.

Inscribed on one side were the words:

AR. NAT. MI.[87]

And, on the other side:

TEM. NA. F.[88]

He urged us not to take anything away with us other than this keepsake.

And so, we went to the sea where our ships were moored, now so richly equipped that it seemed impossible for the equipment not to have been brought over previously.

There were twelve ships now; six of ours and six of the old lord's, which were carrying well-appointed soldiers. However, he came over and joined us on our ship.

The first of the ships carried a great number of the old man's musicians and they sailed out first in order to keep us entertained on the long passage.

Our flags were the twelve signs of the zodiac and we sat in Libra.

As well as the other wonderful things, our ship had a fine and interesting clock, which displayed the time to the minute.

The sea was as calm as could be and it was a pleasure to sail. But what made the journey even more special was the old man's conversation. We passed the time hearing his many wonderful stories and I would be content to spend my entire life listening to him.

Meanwhile, the ships cruised speedily onwards and even before we had sailed for two hours, our sailor told us that he had just seen the whole lake covered in ships. We guessed that they had come to meet us, which turned out to be correct. For as soon as we sailed from the sea and along the river towards the lake, we saw five hundred ships before us! One sparkled with gold and precious stones and, sat within, was the King and Queen together with other lords, ladies and maidens of noble birth.

As soon as we drew near, the cannons fired a salute from both sides, there was such a blare of trumpets, bassoons, and kettledrums that all of the ships rocked about on the water.

At last, as we drew near, our ships were brought alongside, anchored and secured together. Old Atlas stepped forward, representing the King and made a short but impressive speech in which he welcomed us and asked whether the royal presents were ready.

The rest of my companions were mightily confused! They had imagined that they alone were needed to resurrect the King. We four did nothing to enlighten them but instead pretended that we were just as baffled as they were.

After Atlas had finished talking our own old man gave a somewhat longer response, wishing the King and Queen every happiness and prosperity and offering a curious little casket. I have no idea what was in it but it was handed over to Cupid, who took it on behalf of the King and Queen.

After the speeches, a volley of cannons was fired. We took up anchor and sailed together for a good while until we came to shore. This turned out to be right by the first gate where I had entered. Gathered on the shore was a great crowd of the King's family together with hundreds of horses.

We came to the shore and disembarked. The King and Queen, in a gesture of great kindness, offered their hands to all of us in turn. We were then expected to mount the horses.

At this point, I must ask the reader not to read the following section as some sort of boastfulness on my part; please give me some credit. If it was not necessary to relate this as part of the story, I would not give details of the honour that I was shown.

We were all distributed amongst the lords with the exception of the old lord and my most unworthy self. The two of us were given a snow-white banner with a red cross and rode alongside the King.

I think I was only chosen because of my age as both of us matched nicely, having long grey beards and hair! I had also fastened the tokens I received earlier to my hat. The young King noticed them.

'So, you got those tokens at the gate did you?' he asked.

'Yes' I humbly replied.

'There is no need to be so formal with me. You *are* my Father after all!' he laughed before asking 'What did you use to buy them with?'

'Water and salt' I answered.

He pondered this for a little while and asked me how I became so wise. I felt confident enough to tell him the story of what happened to my bread and about the dove and raven. He was delighted with the story and said that he considered God had specifically chosen me to be successful.

We arrived at the first gate where the porter with the blue clothes was waiting. He held a petition. When he saw that I was with the King he handed the petition to me and begged me to put in a good word to the King on his behalf and mention how well he had treated me.

I turned to the King and asked him about the porter's situation. He answered me in a friendly tone and said that the porter was a very famous and outstanding astrologer, who had always been held in high regard by the King's father. However, he made the mistake of going to look at Venus as she was in bed. His punishment was to wait at the first gate for as long as it took until someone released him.

I jumped straight in and said 'May he be released then, please?'

'Yes,' said the King 'provided that someone can be found who has committed an offence at the same level. In that case, he will take his place and we can set this man free'.

This went straight to my heart. My conscience told me that I was such an offender. However, I remained silent and simply handed the petition to the King.

He read it and looked shocked. So much so that the Queen (who was riding behind us with our maidens and another queen; the one from the hanging of the weights) noticed and asked him what was in the letter.

However, he ignored this and put the paper away, changing the subject to other matters of conversation. And so, we rode until around three o'clock, when we arrived at the castle. We dismounted and accompanied the King straight into the hall.

He immediately called for Old Atlas and took him to one side to show him the petition. Atlas left straight away to ride to the porter and find out more about the matter.

After this, the King together with his wife and the other lords, ladies and maidens, sat down. Our Maiden began a speech, highly commending our work, praising the attention to detail we had shown and the suffering we had undergone. She requested that we should all be given a royal reward and that she might also receive the benefits due to her. Next, the old lord stood and backed up everything the Maiden had said, commenting that it was only right that she and we should be recognised for our work. We were asked to come forward and the King addressed us. It was decided that each man would be granted whatever he asked for, within reason. Furthermore, we would make these requests after supper and it was assumed that wise men such as us would be able to ask for something sensible.

In the meantime, the King and Queen began to play some type of board game. It looked similar to chess but the rules were quite different and it was played as 'virtues' against 'vices'. It was fascinating to watch as the vices set traps for the virtues and the virtues avoided and countered them. It was so compelling and cleverly done that I wish we could have the same game for ourselves.

During the game, Atlas returned and reported his findings in private to the King. I went red in the face, as I still felt guilty about the whole thing.

After this, the King handed the petition to me to read and the contents were pretty much as expected:

First, the porter wished the King prosperity and that the royal line be spread far and wide. Then, he said that he considered that the time had come for his release, as promised. For he had discovered that Venus had been uncovered by one of the guests. Of this, he was certain.

He humbly requested that if the King would make a thorough

investigation, he would find that she had been uncovered. If it was found not to be the case however, the porter was happy to continue with his duties at the gate for the rest of his life.

Then he politely requested that, completely at his own risk, he might be permitted to attend the supper this evening, where he hoped to find the offender and therefore secure his own freedom.

It was all well written and carefully calculated. He was clearly a very clever man. But it was far too barbed for me and I wished that I had never read it.

I wondered whether he could be released some other way, perhaps through my wish, so I asked the King.

'No,' he replied 'because this is a special case. However, I don't see why he can't have one evening off to attend the supper'.

With this, he sent someone off to fetch the porter. The tables were prepared for supper in a large room, which we had not seen before. It was so well designed and set out that I am at a loss to describe it adequately. We were conducted into the room with the usual ceremony. I was informed that Cupid would not be present this time as he was fuming about the disgrace that had once again been done to his mother.

In short, the petition (which was my own fault) had caused quite an air of sadness in the room and the King was finding it very awkward to start making enquiries among his guests. It was made worse because asking about it would reveal what had happened, which at the present time was known only to me and him. So, when the porter arrived he told him to carry out the investigation but to do so discreetly. In the meantime, the King put on a brave face and tried to lift everyone's spirits.

Eventually, the mood lifted and everyone began to chat happily. I will not describe the ceremonies and details of the meal as it is not relevant to the story but I will say that 'a good time was had by all' and the conversations were even better than the drink! It turned out to be the last and finest meal at which I was present.

Following the banquet, the chairs were removed and some beautiful armchairs placed in a circle. All of us, together with the King, Queen, both old men, ladies and maidens were directed to sit.

A handsome page opened the beautiful little book and Atlas stood in the middle and addressed us:

He declared that his royal majesty had not forgotten the great service we had performed for him and how well each of us had attended to our duties. As a reward for our services, he had elected us as Knights of the Golden Stone. We were required to make ourselves available for further service and to swear to uphold the associated regulations, so that the King would look upon us favourably.

On this, he ordered the Page to read the regulations:

1. As a knight, you swear never to credit the work of this order to any devil or spirit but only to God, your creator and His handmaid, nature.

2. You will despise all debauchery, pleasure-seeking and uncleanliness and will not bring the order into disrepute.
3. You will use your skills to assist any worthy person in need.
4. You will not use this honour for personal gain.
5. You will not live longer than God wants you to.

We couldn't help but laugh at the final vow and suspected it had been added on as a joke!

After swearing on the King's sceptre, we were knighted with all the usual ceremony. Amongst our privileges was a remit to work to relieve ignorance, poverty and sickness by whatever means we wished. This was validated in a service conducted in a little chapel and we gave our thanks to God. In honour of God, I hung my Golden Fleece and hat in the chapel as an eternal memorial.

And because everyone had to write his name there, I wrote this:

The highest wisdom is to know nothing[89].

Brother Christian Rosencreutz

Knight of the Golden Stone

A.D. 1459.[90]

The others wrote similar things, whatever they felt was appropriate. Afterwards, we were brought back to the hall and seated. We were warned to have our requests ready.

The King and his companions went off into a smaller room in order to hear our wishes. Then we were called in separately, so every man's wish was kept private. Personally, I thought that the most commendable thing I could do after having received such an honour was to demonstrate virtue. I felt that the most appropriate virtue and the one that had given me the most trouble in the past, was gratitude. I know that I could have asked for something special or beneficial to myself but I put any selfish thoughts aside and decided that I would try to free the porter who had helped me, whatever the cost to myself.

As I was called in, I was first of all asked whether, having read the petition, I had seen or had any suspicions as to who the culprit might be? This was my cue and I clearly and carefully told them of everything that had happened, explaining how my ignorance had been responsible for my mistake. I concluded by accepting full responsibility and said that I would take any consequences.

The King and the rest of the lords were quite taken aback by my confession. They asked me to withdraw whilst they conferred.

I was called in again and addressed by Atlas, who once again spoke on the King's behalf:

'The King deeply regrets that you, whom he loves most dearly, has been so unlucky. However much he would like to pardon you, he is bound by the ancient rules. As a result, the porter must be freed and you must take his place. He hopes that someone else guilty of the same offence might one day be discovered and you may go home. However, this is not likely to happen until the wedding feast of his own son'. The verdict nearly killed me and at first, I hated myself and my big mouth. Then I got a grip of myself and found my courage. I thought there was nothing left to lose so I told them how the porter had given me a token and recommended me to the next porter; how he in turn assisted me and caused me to be measured on the scales. Without their help, I would not have been able to experience all of the wonderful things and been so highly honoured. I told them how it was only right that I should show my gratitude by the only means available to me. I thanked them for their judgment and said that I was willing to take the burden for the sake of one who had done so much for me.

I concluded with this:

'My request, if it can be granted, is to be back at my home. If, by my actions, the porter may be free and by my wish I might be freed, then this is what I ask for'.

Unfortunately, this was too much of a stretch but I was told that I could wish for the porter's freedom. The King was most pleased that I had been so honourable but commented that he did not think I realized just what a mess my curiosity had gotten me into. Finally, he declared that the porter was now free and with a heavy heart, I stepped aside. After me, the others were called in. They came out happily, which caused me great pain as I imagined that there was nothing left for me but to live out my days under the gate. My head buzzed with negative thoughts: 'What do I do?', 'How will I pass the time?' Eventually, I came to the conclusion that I was an old man and did not have many years left in me. Plus, all this worrying and unhappiness would see me off sooner rather than later. At least that would mean my door keeping would be at an end and I could then sleep happily in my grave.

I had many thoughts like these. Sometimes, it upset me to think that I had seen such noble things, only to have them taken away. At other times, I was joyful that I had been given so much in my lifetime and was not leaving in disgrace. All of this was the last, and worst, shock that I had to endure.

Whilst I was mulling this over, the others had got ready. The King and lords said goodnight to them and they were taken to their rooms.

But I, in my wretched state, had nobody to escort me and had only torment to endure. To make my new status clear, I had to put on the ring previously worn by the porter.

Finally, the King spoke to me, saying that it was the last time I was likely to see him on these terms and in the future I should behave myself according to my place and not to let down the order. He hugged me warmly and kissed me. I took this as a signal that I was to sit at the gate from tomorrow morning.

The others also spoke to me for a while and shook my hand, wishing me God's blessing.

I was escorted out by the Lord of the Tower and Atlas then taken to a glorious room! There were three beds in the room and each of us took one, spending almost two…

At this point there are at least two remaining pages that are missing. A descriptive note reads:

> 'Here are wanting about two leaves in quarto; and he (the author hereof) whereas he imagined he must in the morning be door-keeper, returned home.'

CHAPTER SEVEN: NOTES

[87] AR. NAT. MI. The marginal notes on the 1616 Strasbourg printing suggest *'Ars naturae ministra'* – Art is the handmaiden of nature

[88] TEM. NA. F. The Strasbourg printing suggests *'Temporis natura filia'* – nature is the daughter of time

[89] Echoes of the Socratic paradox 'I know one thing; that I know nothing' (Usually given in the Latin form as *'ipse se nihil scire id unum sciat'*)

[90] Summa scientia nihil scire

Fr. CHRISTIANUS ROSENCREUTZ,

Eques aurei Lapisis

Anno 1459

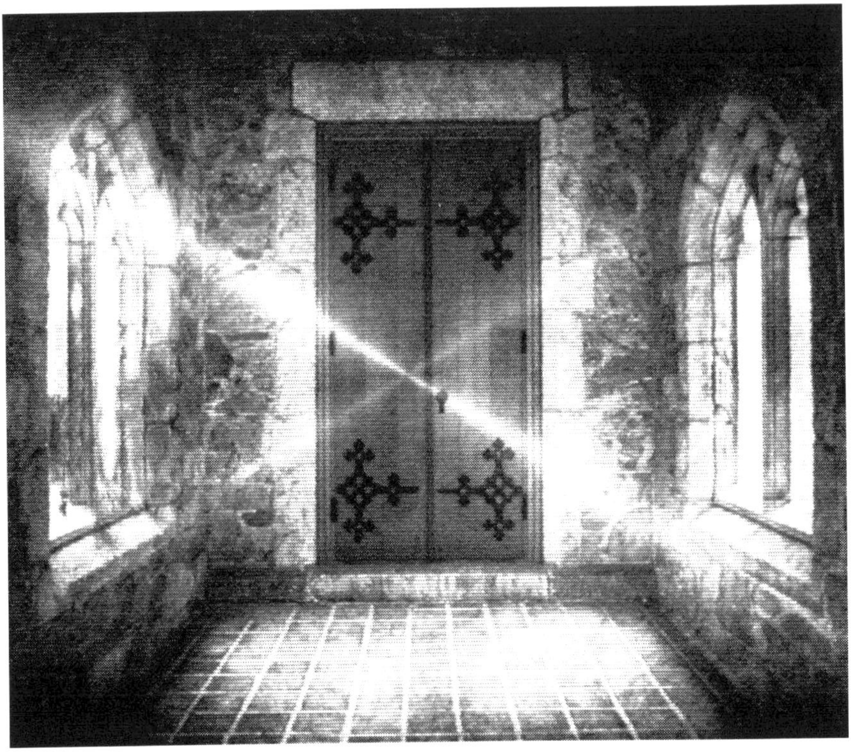

Chapter Eight

The Eighth Day?

'Here are wanting about two leaves in quarto; and he (the author hereof) whereas he imagined he must in the morning be door-keeper, returned home.'

We can only speculate what the missing pages held and how the story of the Chemical Wedding ends. It seems unlikely from the preceding narrative that our hero would complete his journey as the new porter and end his days there.

In several instances before this, he has encountered what he perceives as a point of failure in his quest (or is teased to think so as a prank by others). Each time he has been redeemed and then advanced in status. I have every reason to believe that a similar situation will occur here, especially as he is treated with hugs and kisses from the King and then shown to a 'glorious room'. This does not seem to be the treatment meted out to one who is being punished.

He also has not had a wish granted, although it is clear that it cannot be used to gain freedom. We must also bear in mind that he is protecting another whose sin is as great (if not greater) than his own – the page who led him to Venus and also looked upon her (as well as actively uncovering her). If this sin is found out, the page's punishment can only be to replace Christian as the porter.

It seems that there will be one final redemption before an ultimate reward for our noble Brother. It is likely to comprise of one final day, making eight in total.

I like to think that the meek shall indeed inherit the Earth.

Rest well Brother Rosencreutz.

Acknowledgements

Any book is rarely the product of a single person. The effort that goes into any work is supplemented and supported by a numerous cast. It is difficult to find appropriate words to truly express due gratitude for those that love, support and put up with us. Sometimes you can be there during the hard times you don't even know about. I hope 'thanks' is sufficient for now.

To the Fratres of the Societas Rosicruciana In Anglia – a sincere thank you for the many happy times and interesting conversations with so many of you over the years. It is the inspiration of the Society and the hope that I can be of some small service to the Fratres that has led me to write this book. May you continue to enjoy the Society as much as I do.

Thank you to Robert Hughes. Your encouragement, friendship and knowledge has always improved the quality of whatever is under discussion and this book would not exist without you.

Finally thanks to those who have helped so many times over the years that I have worked on this book. Whether it has been encouragement, information, opinion, or just a kind word or chat that has cheered me up at the right time, you have probably helped me at times more than you know and I am indebted to you for your friendship and kindness.

So, a grateful thank you to Julia, Susan and David Markham. Prof Sylvester Arnab, Kenneth Doyle, Kirst D'Raven, Jamie Ekin, Dr Andy Fear, Prof Phil Harris, Chris & Sian Lawlor, Val Price, Carrie Searley, Stephen Volk and Harry Wright for making this all possible.

Printed in Great Britain
by Amazon